Practice Companion
VOLUME 2

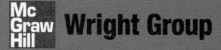

McGraw Hill Wright Group

www.WrightGroup.com

Send all inquiries to:
Wright Group/McGraw-Hill
P.O. Box 812960
Chicago, IL 60681

ISBN 978-0-07-656541-2
MHID 0-07-656541-6

3 4 5 6 7 8 9 RMN 16 15 14 13 12 11

The McGraw·Hill Companies

Contents

Unit 5

Unit 6

Selection 3

Focus Question

What happens when there are changes to an ecosystem?

Selection 4

Focus Question

How do people play a part in ecosystems?

Unit 7

Unit 8

Selection ③

Focus Question

How do people stick with their goals, even when they face challenges?

Selection ④

Focus Question

What does it feel like to achieve something you've worked hard for?

My Weekly Planner

Week of _____

Theme Vocabulary	This week's words:
Differentiated Vocabulary	This week's words:
Comprehension Strategy and Skill	This week's comprehension strategy: This week's comprehension skill:
Vocabulary Strategy	This week's vocabulary strategy:
Spelling/Word Study Skill	This week's spelling skill:
Word Study Skill	This week's word study skill:
Fluency	This week's fluency selection:
Writing and Language Arts	This week's writing form:
Grammar	This week's grammar skills:

Word Origins and Meanings

Read the words, their definitions, and the information about the sources of the words. Write a sentence using each word in the bottom part of each square.

Basin

Definition: all the land that is drained by a river and the streams that run into that river

Source: from Latin *bacca* meaning "water vessel"

Sentence:

Landform

Definition: a natural feature of the land

Source: compound word = land + form

Sentence:

Transport

Definition: to carry or bring from one place to another

Source: from Latin *trans* meaning "over" and *portare* meaning "to carry"

Sentence:

Flourish

Definition: to grow or develop strongly

Source: from Old French *florir* meaning "to flower"

Sentence:

Related Words

Follow the directions for each numbered item below.

1. Since Erik learned the meaning of *basin,* whenever he thinks of rivers, *basin* is a word that he relates to rivers. List three more words that you relate to rivers. Then list four words for each of the other bodies of water.

river *basin.* _____

_____

ocean _____

_____

lake _____

_____

2. Liz is trying to list all the *landforms* she can. She has just begun the list. What *landforms* can you add? Write three examples below.

mountains _____

_____

3. Jorge lives in a big city. He is thinking of all the different means of *transport* that exist in his city. What words can you add to his list?

subway, trucks, cabs. _____

_____

4. Marta thinks that many things can *flourish,* not just plants. Help her explain her idea by finishing the sentences below.

Towns flourish when they _____

_____

Schoolchildren flourish when they _____

_____

Businesses flourish when they _____

_____

Words with *k, ng,* and *kw* Sounds

			Frequently misspelled words	Review words
risky	junk	blank		
blanket	mistake	monkey	before	spied
picnic	topic	public		families
banker	pocket	earthquake	knew	
electric	equal			
question	attack			

A Write each word and draw a line between the syllables in each word.

1. r i s k y _____

2. e l e c t r i c _____

3. t o p i c _____

4. b l a n k e t _____

5. q u e s t i o n _____

6. p o c k e t _____

7. m o n k e y _____

8. p i c n i c _____

9. e q u a l _____

10. p u b l i c _____

11. b a n k e r _____

12. m i s t a k e _____

13. a t t a c k _____

14. e a r t h q u a k e _____

B Look at the words you wrote in Activity A. Circle the letters in each answer that make the *k, ng,* or *kw* sounds.

C **Read the paragraph. Circle the misspelled words and then write the words correctly on the lines below.**

> Befor he left for the company picknic, michael made sure that he had everything. He packed the blancket and remembered to put the camera in his poket. When he got to the publik park, the other banckers were already there. He set his stuff down and went over to see what the topik of conversation was. His friends were talking about the latest riscky investments and some of the mistaces that people had made after the big earthkwake last week. Michael new that electrik companies were still trying to get power back to a lot of people and kwuestioned how long it would take for everyone to have power again. The amount of money being spent to repair the damage was ekwal to almost $50,000! He hoped that there wouldn't be another earthquake again as they were so expensive to clean up after.

1. _____

2. _____

3. _____

4. _____

5. _____

6. _____

7. _____

8. _____

9. _____

10. _____

11. _____

12. _____

13. _____

14. _____

15. Which word in the above paragraph should be capitalized? _____

Newspaper Article

Practice reading this newspaper article to a partner.

Homestead Act Signed

by Ronald Enfield

May 20, 1862

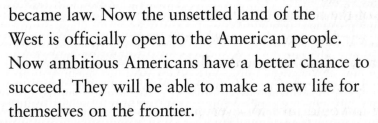

WASHINGTON—On this momentous day, the Homestead Act, signed by President Abraham Lincoln, became law. Now the unsettled land of the West is officially open to the American people. Now ambitious Americans have a better chance to succeed. They will be able to make a new life for themselves on the frontier.

The West is ideal for farming. It has vast stretches of flat, fertile grassland. There is an abundance of rain each year. Possibilities are everywhere in this untapped area. Settlers will have their pick of crops to plant. The rich soil is accommodating to all types of plant life.

The Homestead Act provides Americans the chance for a new start. With hard work and determination, individuals can cultivate and develop their plots of land. They can build a better life for the generations to come. The rich, fertile farmland of the West is going fast. Don't miss out! A fresh start is waiting for you!

Did you read the newspaper article with fluency? Use the form on the next page to evaluate yourself and your partner.

Reading Response Form

A On a scale of 1 to 5, rate yourself and your partner. Do this for the first reading and final readings, at least. On a scale of 1 to 5, 5 is considered outstanding, 3 is good, and 1 is average.

1. Did I ...

	First Reading	Second Reading	Final Reading
Read the words correctly?			
Read at a good pace?			
Read with expression?			
Read clearly for my audience?			

2. Did my partner ...

	First Reading	Second Reading	Final Reading
Read the words correctly?			
Read at a good pace?			
Read with expression?			
Read clearly for the audience?			

B After the first reading, share with your partner how you thought he or she read, and offer suggestions for improvement.

C After the final reading, answer the following questions for yourself.

1. What did I do well?

First Reading _____

Second Reading _____

Final Reading _____

2. What should I do to improve my reading next time?

First Reading _____

Second Reading _____

Final Reading _____

Visualize

When you **visualize** while reading, you:

- Use the text to picture things in your mind

- Put together your experiences with what you have read

When you visualize something, you try to experience it. You should try to use all five senses. Ask yourself the following questions:

- What does it look like?

- What does it sound like?

- What does it feel like?

- What can I smell or taste?

Look at the passage below. The sensory details have been underlined.

Mom and I had heard about Capri, but this island off of Italy turned out to be more beautiful than we had imagined. The white rock isle rises up from an incredibly blue sea. From high atop the island, the view is stunning. Old buildings have colorful paintings on the sides. Shops are everywhere, and the smells of sweet flowers and delicious foods fill the air.

The town bustles with all kinds of people. Everyone can enjoy a great meal of bread, fresh olives, and fresh fish while sitting in the warm sunshine.

Close your eyes and picture what is described. Can you visualize the Isle of Capri?

Read the passage below. As you read, look for details that appeal to your senses. Then answer the questions.

After a forced march from Alabama in 1836, Creek Indians reached what is now Oklahoma. Settling near a cool, fast-flowing river, they called their new home "Tulsee."

Now called Tulsa, this city began to flourish when oil was found in 1901. Today, Tulsa is also known for its art centers, universities, and gardens. The sweet smell of roses in a famous garden is one thing many visitors remember most about their trip to Tulsa.

Tulsa is also a transportation center. The sounds of trains, buses, trucks, and airplanes create a daily roar in the city. If you like traveling by boat, you can go from Tulsa all the way to the Great Lakes or the Gulf of Mexico.

Don't be in a hurry to leave Tulsa, though. Take the time to enjoy a delicious hamburger, a favorite local food. If you are not fond of hamburgers you can always enjoy the pickle bar at one favorite restaurant!

1. When you visualize Tulsa, what can you see in your mind?

_____

2. When you visualize Tulsa, what do you hear?

_____

3. When you visualize Tulsa, what tastes and smells come to mind?

_____

Antonyms

> **Antonyms** are words that have opposite meanings.
> In order to be antonyms, the two words must be the
> same part of speech.

You can quickly learn the meaning of an unfamiliar word if you
know it is an antonym for a word that you know. Sometimes a
writer gives you a clue that words are antonyms. These clue words
usually show contrast such as *but*, *on the other hand*, or *rather*.

Look at the example below.

> **Some people detest hot *humid* weather *but***
> **enjoy the *dry* heat of the desert.**

If you did not know the meaning of the word *humid*,
you could tell from the writer's clue, *but*, that this
word means the opposite of *dry*.

At other times the context of what you read helps you figure out
that a new word is an antonym for a known word.

Look at the example below.

> **After hiking halfway up the mountain, I was very**
> **hot and extremely tired. The *gorgeous* view at**
> **the top, however, made me forget all about the**
> **tough hike. I was so thrilled I had made it!**

As you try to figure out the meaning of the word
gorgeous, you might think to yourself: "Few people would
be thrilled to see an ugly view. *Gorgeous* must mean the
opposite of *ugly*."

Read the word in the center of each web. Fill in the circles surrounding each word with antonyms. Remember that antonyms must be the same part of speech. If you need help, use a thesaurus to look up antonyms.

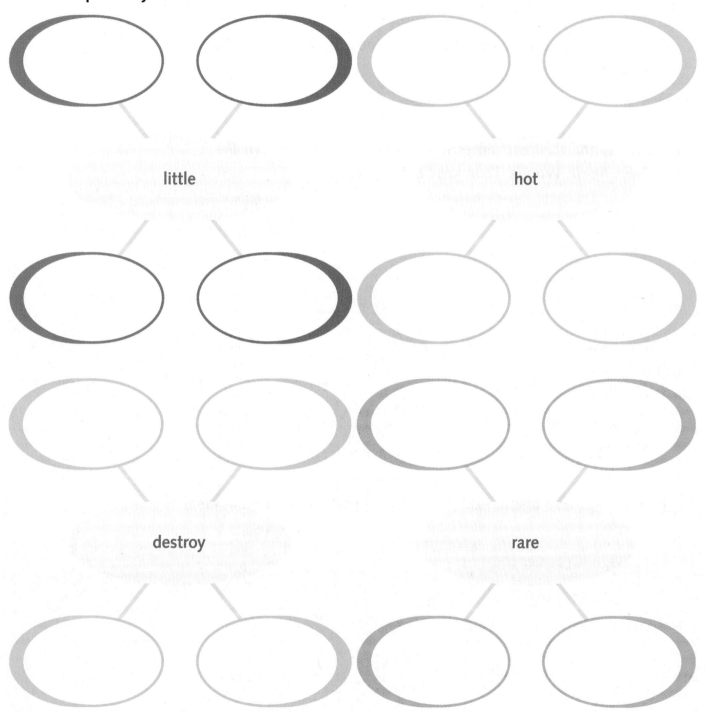

little

hot

destroy

rare

Identify Main Idea and Details

When you read, think about the **main idea**, or the most important part of a selection. Then try to find those **details** that best support, or help explain, the main idea.

To find the main idea, ask yourself:

> **What is this selection about? What does the author want me to know?**

A Look at the students' notes from page 298 of *Marven of the Great North Woods.* Then answer the questions.

Marven learns about the bookkeeping system.	cord chits=number of cords cut symbol=a worker's mark	doublees=two workers per chit triplees=three workers per chit

1. What does the first note tell? _____

2. What do the second and third notes tell? _____

B Read page 298 again. Add details to support the new main idea.

Marven improves the bookkeeping system.		

Prefixes That Tell *Where*

The following **prefixes** can describe *where:*

ex-   a-   re-

intro-   mid-   trans-

If you see a word with one of the above prefixes, that word is most likely telling about where something is.

Ⓐ Use your knowledge of prefixes to complete the sentences with the correct word from the box. The first one has been done for you.

introduction	recross	explore
apart	midstream	transatlantic

1. When my grandfather came to the United States, he took a
   transatlantic ship from Italy.

2. We left from opposite banks and waded until we met
   midstream by a rock.

3. She left her hometown to _explore_ the
   world and see new people and places.

4. I learned a lot about the author's life by reading the
   introduction at the front of the book.

5. The towns were ten miles _apart_
   and connected by the highway.

6. He would need to _recross_ the train
   tracks if he took the same route back home.

Ⓑ Write a sentence that uses a word with a *mid-* or *trans-* prefix.

I go to therapy midweek every
week.

Inquiry Checklist: Week 1

Put a check mark next to each item once it is complete.

Discussion Roles

☐ I took a role in my group.

PRACTICE COMPANION 370

My role is _____.

---

1. Generate Ideas and Questions

☐ We thought of at least three possible questions.

☐ We chose an Inquiry Question to investigate.

---

2. Make a Conjecture

☐ We shared what we know about our Inquiry Question.

☐ We made a conjecture about our Inquiry Question.

☐ We filled in the Idea Tracker for Week 1.

☐ We posted our Inquiry Question and conjecture on the Question Board.

---

3. Make Plans to Collect Information

☐ We made a list of topics to research and split them up among the group.

☐ We used the Information Finder and made a list of possible sources to use.

PRACTICE COMPANION 371

☐ All group members completed their Week 1 Inquiry Planners.

PRACTICE COMPANION 15

Notes:

_____

_____

_____

_____

Inquiry Planner: Week 1

Write your group's Inquiry Question and conjecture. Then write your Action Plan for next week.

My group's Inquiry Question is: _____

_____

My group's conjecture is: _____

_____

Action Plan

1. What topics will I collect information for? _____

_____

_____

2. What sources will I use? _____

_____

_____

3. Where will I find these sources? _____

_____

_____

4. When will I collect information? _____

_____

5. How will I record the information? _____

_____

_____

Mural

Read about murals and study the example.

What Is a Mural?

- A mural is a large illustration that shows a concept or tells a story.

- It may show one or several scenes.

- It is usually in a public place where everyone can see it.

- A mural may be drawn or painted.

You Can Use Technology

Find out how technology can help you create and share your presentation.

- Log on to **www.wgLEAD21.com.**

- From My Home Page, click on Inquiry Project.

Focus Question: How are geography and economy connected in the Midwest?

Think about what you read in your selection. Using what you learned, how do you think geography and economy are connected in the Midwest? Fill in the chart below with your answers.

Geography	Economy

What makes the Central Region special? Use examples from your selection to explain your answer on the lines below.

_____

_____

_____

_____

_____

_____

_____

Focus Question: How are geography and economy connected in the South Central States?

Think about the following three things: *rivers*, *mountains*, and *plains*. In what ways are these geographical features connected to the economy of the South Central States? Write your answers on the lines below.

Rivers _____

_____

_____

Mountains _____

_____

_____

Plains _____

_____

_____

My Weekly Planner

Week of _____

Theme Vocabulary	This week's words:
Differentiated Vocabulary	This week's words:
Comprehension Strategy and Skill	This week's comprehension strategy: This week's comprehension skill:
Vocabulary Strategy	This week's vocabulary strategy:
Spelling/Word Study Skill	This week's spelling skill:
Word Study Skill	This week's word study skill:
Fluency	This week's fluency selection:
Writing and Language Arts	This week's writing form:
Grammar	This week's grammar skills:

Making Word Connections

Fill in the charts below with words that come to mind when you think of the vocabulary words for this week.

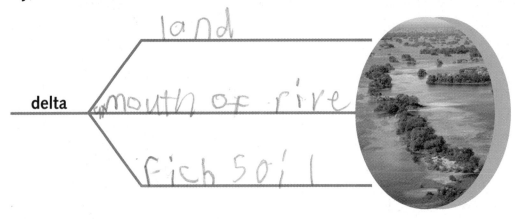

delta — land / mouth of river / rich soil

diverse — diffrenlt / several / unlike

Use the definitions to form sentences that use the vocabulary words correctly. You can use the words from the charts in your sentences.

1. **delta:** an area of land at the mouth of a river, formed by mud, sand, and pebble deposits

   _____

   _____

2. **diverse:** different from one another; not all the same

   _____

   _____

Using Context Clues

Read the passage below. Then follow the instructions next to each numbered item below.

The Delta

People who live in Mississippi call one big area of their state "the Delta." This area is where the banks of the mighty Mississippi River overflow, leaving rich, fertile soil behind.

Farmers in the Delta grow all types of crops. All of the rice grown in Mississippi comes from this region. The fertile soil yields plenty of other foods as well.

People enjoy the diverse activities that they can do in the Delta. Dams along the Mississippi River have created large reservoirs. Other lakes, called oxbow lakes, were made by the river itself, when it shifted course. Swimming and kayaking are just two of the fun activities people engage in on these lakes.

1. The passage uses the words *rich* and *fertile* to describe the land in the Delta. List other words that might describe the soil. Think about its color and its texture.

   _____

2. In paragraph 2, which words or phrases could be replaced by the vocabulary word *diverse*?

   _____

3. What are other "diverse" activities you could do in the Delta?

   _____

Words with Final *j* and *s* Sounds

			Frequently misspelled words	Review words
twice	since	judge		
practice	edge	stage		monkey
package	glance	office	their	
bridge	marriage	chance		public
notice	baggage		though	
message	manage			

A **Read the sentences below. Write the correct spelling of each misspelled word. The first one has been done for you.**

1. We walked across the bridje late last night.
   bridge

2. Her glanse fell on me as she looked around the room.
   _____

3. Did Al give you my mesaje? _____

4. The airline lost my bagage. _____

5. The ofice is always quiet at this time of night.
   _____

6. The ege of the desk is sharp. _____

7. The staje was beautifully decorated for the show.
   _____

8. Sinse when do you ride the bus to school?
   _____

9. Sarah returned the pacage to the post office.
   _____

B The paragraph below contains misspellings of fourteen of this week's spelling words. Find the errors, circle them, and write the correct spelling of each word on the lines below.

I can't wait for my chanse to act in the school play! It is almost perfect, but we still need to practise the last scene. We ran through the scene twise, but Mr. Greco, our director, thinks it still needs work sinse it's not quite right yet. This scene is difficult because we all need to imagine we are standing on a brige as we celebrate the marrije of Sir John Whitbread III and Lady Deerwood. The staj is very small and during there wedding scene, the actress playing Lady Deerwood almost fell off the eje. Mr. Greco was so focused on the scene he did not seem to notise (but I think he did manaje to see it when he glansed up). I hope that he is pleased with everything. When I got backstage on opening night, there was a good luck messagge from him on his offise door. We are so excited to show our play to the school!

1. _____

2. _____

3. _____

4. _____

5. _____

6. _____

7. _____

8. _____

9. _____

10. _____

11. _____

12. _____

13. _____

14. _____

Advertisement

Practice reading this advertisement to a partner.

Come to the Coast!

Have you had enough of cold, icy winters? Tired of living where snow falls for half the year? Want to throw away that snow shovel? If you answered "Yes!" to any of these questions, then we know of just the place for you—the Gulf Coast!

The Gulf Coast is one of America's most appealing and attractive regions. Our vibrant waterways give you hundreds of ways to enjoy your time here. Enjoy the majestic scenery along the banks of the Mighty Mississippi. Spend your days fishing or shrimping. Or relax on a leisurely boat ride along the gorgeous Gulf of Mexico.

Since the Gulf Coast states are on the water, shipping is also a major industry. Two of the region's largest ports—Houston and New Orleans—are brimming with history, culture, and entertainment. Music fans can soak up the soulful sounds of New Orleans jazz music in the historic French Quarter. Hungry visitors can also enjoy traditional dishes like gumbo and jambalaya.

So head to the Gulf Coast and get ready to experience a lovely and lively lifestyle!

Did you read the advertisement with fluency? Use the form on the next page to evaluate yourself and your partner.

Reading Response Form

A On a scale of 1 to 5, rate yourself and your partner. Do this for the first reading and final readings, at least. On a scale of 1 to 5, 5 is considered outstanding, 3 is good, and 1 is average.

1. Did I …

	First Reading	Second Reading	Final Reading
Read the words correctly?			
Read at a good pace?			
Read with expression?			
Read clearly for my audience?			

2. Did my partner …

	First Reading	Second Reading	Final Reading
Read the words correctly?			
Read at a good pace?			
Read with expression?			
Read clearly for the audience?			

B After the first reading, share with your partner how you thought he or she read, and offer suggestions for improvement.

C After the final reading, answer the following questions for yourself.

1. What did I do well?

First Reading _____

Second Reading _____

Final Reading _____

2. What should I do to improve my reading next time?

First Reading _____

Second Reading _____

Final Reading _____

Monitor Comprehension

Good readers **monitor their comprehension.** They check to make sure they understand what they are reading. If a reader does not understand something, he or she might:

- Adjust reading pace or reread the text

- Read on for more information

- Ask someone for help

Good readers check to see how well they understand a text. For example, good readers might stop after each paragraph to make sure they understood what they have just read.

Questions that help readers monitor comprehension include:

- What is the main idea of this paragraph?

- What should I remember about this page?

- Are there any words that I could not figure out?

- What does the illustration or photo tell me about the text?

- How does _____ work?

- How does _____ look?

- How does _____ act?

- How could I describe this idea to someone else?

Sometimes rereading a difficult section of text can help. If you know you need to understand it better, you can read more carefully for clues to its meaning.

Read this selection from a larger text. Then answer the questions.

Minnesota has many nicknames. Each nickname tells something different about the state. The nickname "Land of 10,000 Lakes," for example, tells people that the state has many lakes, rivers, and ponds. These bodies of water were left behind by ancient glaciers.

The nickname "Bread and Butter State" tells us about two important industries in Minnesota. Many dairy farms are located in the state and food processing plants in the state produce tons of butter and cheese. In addition, wheat farming leads to the production of plenty of bread.

Minnesota's official nickname, however, is the "North Star State." Other than Alaska, no state in the United States is farther north than Minnesota, making this nickname very appropriate.

1. You do not understand the last sentence of the first paragraph. You reread the paragraph, but it does not help. You glance ahead through the text and see that there is a section on Minnesota's 10,000-year-old history. You decide to read on. Why is this a good strategy?

_____

2. During your first read, the last sentence of paragraph 2 does not seem to fit. You reread the paragraph. Does this strategy help you better understand why this sentence is included?

_____

3. You have heard of the North Star, but you do not remember much about it. You decide to look it up. Why?

_____

Using a Thesaurus

> A **thesaurus** is a reference book that lists synonyms and, sometimes, antonyms. It presents words in a way that lets you see word relationships and helps you to understand the various meanings of words.

To look up a word in a thesaurus, you would first go to the thesaurus's **index**. The index tells you the entry number in the thesaurus where you can find the word. It also helps you decide which entry word would be best.

For example, you look up the word *little* in the index and find this:

little   -in quantity   53

            -in size   187

Since you are looking for a word to describe the size of something, you turn to entry 187. There, you find the word *little* listed with 25 synonyms. You choose *puny* as the perfect word for your size description.

> Looking up a new word in a thesaurus gives you different information than what you find in a dictionary. A *dictionary* tells the word's meaning. A *thesaurus* helps you see how the word relates to other words. It makes the meaning clearer.

You learn from the dictionary, for example, that *sufficient* means "enough." From the thesaurus, you get a better sense of how much "enough" is when you see these synonyms listed: *adequate, competent, satisfactory, ample, plenty, abundant.*

You now understand that getting "sufficient rainfall" in an area means that there is more than enough rain to keep the soil moist.

Read the example below. Answer the questions that follow.

1. Ava was reading about someone who had a *buoyant* personality. She looked up *buoyant* in the dictionary and learned that it means "cheerful." Now she is looking *buoyant* up in the thesaurus. Which entry should she turn to? Circle your answer.

     buoyant   -floating   312

                -hopeful   872

2. Once at the entry, Ava finds these synonyms: *hopeful, confident, secure, elated,* and *enthusiastic.* Where can she look to see a list of antonyms?

_____

_____

3. Ava thinks she has located the antonyms list. It begins with the word *hopeless.* Is this the right entry? Why or why not?

_____

_____

_____

4. Think of a time when you have felt buoyant. Describe that time using the word *buoyant* and at least two synonyms from the thesaurus list above.

_____

_____

_____

_____

_____

_____

Identify Main Idea and Details

The main idea is the most important idea in a selection.

Supporting details provide information about the main idea to explain it.

Think about a place that you like, such as your room or a place you often visit. In the chart below, write down the reason why you like this place and the details that explain your reason.

Main Idea

The cabin

Supporting Detail

because the cabin has a hottub inside

Supporting Detail

To see people go down the big slide

Supporting Detail

Family

30

Greek and Latin Roots

Many words have roots that come from Greek and Latin words. When you see these words, you can figure out their meanings by recalling what the root word means. Some common Greek and Latin roots include:

> *phon* "sound"   *spec* and *vid* "see"   *sign* "mark"
>
> *photo* "light"   *graph* "write"   *mot* "move"

Use your knowledge of Greek and Latin roots to choose the word from the box that best completes each sentence.

emotion	inspector	biography
video	photographer	signal
megaphone		

1. The _____ went through the building and looked for any problems in its construction.

2. I knew when the catcher gave the hand _____ for a fastball that the visiting team was out of luck.

3. I wish I had captured the game on _____ so I could watch it again.

4. A _____ from the newspaper took pictures of the visiting officials.

5. All the fans leapt to their feet with great _____ after the amazing catch.

6. My brother belted a loud "Hooray" into his _____.

7. She said it was a complete _____ of Gandhi, but the book only focused on a few years in his life.

31

Inquiry Checklist: Week 2

Put a check mark next to each item once it is complete.

Collect Information

☐ I used the Evaluating Sources Checklist to check my sources.
PRACTICE COMPANION 372

☐ I recorded information from at least one good source using an Investigation Sheet.

4. Organize and Synthesize Information

☐ Each person in my group shared information.

☐ We organized the information using the Chain Organizer or another type of organizer.

☐ We synthesized the information and found at least one new idea.

5. Confirm or Revise Your Conjecture

☐ We used our new understandings to decide if we should revise our conjecture or our Inquiry Question.

☐ We filled in the Idea Tracker for Week 2.

☐ We posted our revised Inquiry Question and conjecture on the Question Board.

☐ All group members completed their Week 2 Inquiry Planners.

PRACTICE COMPANION 33

Notes:

_____

_____

_____

_____

_____

Inquiry Planner: Week 2

Write your group's updated Inquiry Question and conjecture. Then write your Action Plan for next week.

My group's updated Inquiry Question is: _____

_____

My group's updated conjecture is: _____

_____

Action Plan

1. What topics will I collect information for?_____

_____

_____

2. What sources will I use? _____

_____

_____

3. Where will I find these sources? _____

_____

_____

4. When will I collect information? _____

_____

_____

5. How will I record the information? _____

_____

_____

Focus Question: How are geography and economy connected in the South Central States?

Based on your selection, what are some ways geography and economy are connected in the South Central States? Fill in the chart with your answers.

Geography	Economy

What makes the Central Region special? Use examples from your selection to explain your answer.

_____

_____

_____

_____

_____

_____

_____

_____

What do you think life was like for children living in the Midwest 150 years ago? What things about their lives might have been difficult? What responsibilities do you think they had? Write your answers on the lines below.

Children had difficulties because _____

_____

_____

_____

Children's responsibilities included _____

_____

_____

_____

Study the Model

Descriptive Essay

Read the Writing Model along with your teacher. Look for the facts and details as well as the precise adjectives.

Harvest Gold

by Will Sheridan

Have you ever stood in the middle of a huge cornfield, right before the corn was about to be harvested? Have you ever felt the gentle wind rushing through the rows and heard the rustling of the green leaves blowing this way and that way? Have you smelled the sweetness of the corn ready to be picked? I have! My family and other farmers in our town grow corn. One sunny day, I stood in our cornfield and enjoyed the sights and sounds of the corn.

When I stood in the cornfield, first I noticed the tall, green plants. They were higher than the top of my head. I ran my hands along each of them, feeling the papery husks of corn. Some stalks were taller than others. Their broad, tough leaves were everywhere I looked. Some were bent by the wind or the hot, strong sun.

My father made sure our rows of corn were planted in straight lines. They almost looked like chairs in a classroom or soldiers in a line.

Each ear of corn looked like a perfectly wrapped present, waiting to be opened. When I held one in my hand, it was warm from the sun beating down on it all day. The green husks covered it tightly, with just one tiny, yellow end peeking out. I wanted to unwrap it, but I didn't. I would wait! I was excited for the corn to grow so I could eat some!

Standing in our cornfield and thinking about the delicious corn that I would have for dinner that night made me hungry. I think our corn is the tastiest corn of all! It made me happy to live in the Midwest. If you have never had a chance to visit a cornfield, I hope you will soon. There is nothing better on a summer afternoon.

Evaluation Rubric

Descriptive Essay

Category	Goals	Yes	Needs Work!	Now it's OK.
Organization	The beginning paragraph tells what the essay is about and grabs the reader's attention. Each middle paragraph provides details about a different part of the subject.			
Ideas	My descriptive essay is interesting for my readers. I include supporting details about each part of the subject.			
Voice	The descriptive essay sounds like I wrote it.			
Word Choice	I use good descriptive language to give the reader a clear picture of my subject.			
Sentence Fluency	I use a variety of sentence types.			
Conventions	I use capital letters at the beginning of each sentence and for all proper nouns. I use correct punctuation. I use pronouns and comparative adjectives correctly. All the words are spelled correctly.			

Descriptive Essay

Peer Review

Read your partner's paper. Then finish each sentence.

1. I see that this descriptive essay is organized with _____

_____

_____

2. Some supporting details that the author uses to describe different

parts of the subject are _____

_____

_____

3. One example of a detail or piece of descriptive language that the

author might use to add interest is _____

_____

_____

Name of Reader _____

Object Pronouns

Object pronouns are used in place of nouns that are not the subject of the sentence. Object pronouns tell *who* or *what* receives the action of the verb.

Singular Object Pronouns	Plural Object Pronouns
me you it	us them
him her	you

A Look at the sentences. Choose the correct pronoun and write it on the line. Then write the word that the pronoun replaces. The first one has been done for you.

1. My cousins are in town, and I saw (us, them) yesterday.
   them, cousins

2. Look at Bryan and his new puppy! He takes (it, he) to the park every day. _it   puppy_

3. Our team invited the minor league players to the game. They like to watch (they, us) play.
   us   Our team

4. Rosa's dress was too long, so she gave (them, it) to me.
   it   dress

5. Claire got the highest grade in the class. The teacher gave (her, she) a prize. _her   claire_

B Write an object pronoun for the underlined word or words.

1. Let's go with <u>Julio and Tony</u>. _them_

2. Bill cooked for <u>Jan and me</u>. _us_

3. Wash <u>the car</u>. _it_

4. I read to <u>Carla</u> each night. _her_

Possessive Pronouns

Possessive pronouns show ownership. They tell the person or people to whom something belongs. Common possessive pronouns are listed below:

Pronouns Used Alone			
mine	yours	his	hers
its	ours	theirs	

Pronouns That Appear Before a Noun			
my	your	his	her
its	our	their	

A Write the correct possessive pronoun on the line.

1. The vase belongs to my mother. It's _hers_.

2. Mr. and Mrs. Morris adopted a kitten. It's _theirs_.

3. We bought a new car. It's _ours_.

4. I got a computer for my birthday. It's _mine_.

5. I knitted you a scarf. It's _yours_.

B Choose the correct pronoun and write it on the line.

1. That's not my dad's car. (Him, His) car is much bigger. _His_

2. The dress fits me because it's (mine, my). _mine_

3. The Andersons borrowed our blender because they could not find (mine, theirs). _theirs_

4. I like his blueberry pie, but (hers, her) tastes better. _hers_

Descriptive Adjectives

Descriptive adjectives tell *what kind, which one,* and *how many.*
When you write, make sure that you use descriptive adjectives
correctly. Remember that adjectives can be written in different parts
of the sentence.

Example 1

- Martha is wearing a red dress.

- I have a friendly dog.

- Scott bought fresh fruit.

Example 2

- Martha's dress is red.

- My dog is friendly.

- The fruit Scott bought is fresh.

Write a sentence for each of the descriptive adjectives below.

coarse	generous	precious
earnest	jolly	rare
fierce	magnificent	scarlet

1. My jeans feel coase.

2. My grandma gives me generous gifts.

3. My green blanket is precious to me.

4. _____

5. _____

6. _____

7. _____

8. _____

9. _____

Adjectives That Compare

Adjectives that compare two or more things often use the suffixes -*er* and -*est*. When you write, it is important that you use these adjectives correctly.

Comparative Adjectives Use -*er*
- My pencil is <u>shorter</u> than yours.
- This path is <u>rockier</u> than the first one.

Superlative Adjectives Use -*est*
- Clay's pencil is the <u>shortest</u>.
- The path by the lake is the <u>rockiest</u> one in the park.

Choose the word that best completes each sentence. Write it on the line. The first one has been done for you.

1. Jogging is (hardest, harder) than walking.
   harder

2. This is the (longer, longest) book I have ever read.
   _____

3. Melissa has the (cleaner, cleanest) desk in the whole school.
   _____

4. What is the (sad, saddest) movie you have ever seen?
   _____

5. Yesterday I felt very sick, but today I feel (healthier, healthiest).
   _____

6. It is (hot, hotter) in the afternoon than it is in the evening.
   _____

7. This bunny is the (softest, softer) toy I have ever felt!
   _____

8. Our classroom is (biggest, bigger) than the Grade 5 classroom.
   _____

Using Test-Taking Strategies

Read this sample question based on *A Tour of the Central Region*.

Sample Question:

Why is the geography of the Central Region important?

Ⓐ The geography is the most beautiful in the United States.
Ⓑ The Central Region has tourist attractions, such as Mount Rushmore.
Ⓒ The geography provides ways for people to earn a living.
Ⓓ This region has waterways, such as the St. Lawrence Seaway.

Why the geography is important has to be proven.

- Is Ⓐ a possible answer? No, because this answer states an opinion, not a fact.

- Is Ⓑ a possible answer? This answer does not have much to do with geography.

- Is Ⓒ a possible answer? This answer states a main idea from the selection and states how the geography affects the people.

- Is Ⓓ a possible answer? No, this answer simply discusses the rivers but not why they are important.

By thinking carefully about each answer choice, and checking back to see what the story says, you can pick the correct answer. In this case, C is the answer.

Applying Test-Taking Strategies

Here are more questions to answer. Look carefully at each answer choice. Cross off the letter of any choice you know is wrong.

1. How do many people in the Great Plains earn a living?

   Ⓐ They sell corn and wheat.
   Ⓑ They sell fish and shellfish.
   Ⓒ They sell produce from their orchards.
   Ⓓ They sell lumber from trees.
   (page 262)

2. Why are canals important to the economy of the Central Region?

   Ⓐ They allow tourists to travel throughout this region.
   Ⓑ They help fertilize the soil so more crops can grow.
   Ⓒ They allow goods to be shipped all over the world.
   Ⓓ They provide people with a place to swim and play.
   (page 263)

3. What is the most likely reason why the Homestead Act of 1862 provided free land?

   Ⓐ The government wanted to honor Lewis and Clark.
   Ⓑ The government wanted the economy to grow.
   Ⓒ The government wanted to build more canals.
   Ⓓ The government wanted to build more assembly lines.
   (pages 266-267)

My Weekly Planner

Week of _____

Theme Vocabulary	This week's words:
Differentiated Vocabulary	This week's words:
Comprehension Strategy and Skill	This week's comprehension strategy: This week's comprehension skill:
Vocabulary Strategy	This week's vocabulary strategy:
Spelling/Word Study Skill	This week's spelling skill:
Word Study Skill	This week's word study skill:
Fluency	This week's fluency selection:
Writing and Language Arts	This week's writing form:
Grammar	This week's grammar skills:

Complete Ideas

Read the definitions and example sentences below that use the vocabulary words.

glide: to move along smoothly

> Swans glide across the pond.

mutter: to speak in a voice that is low and not clear

> My grandmother told me to speak up and not to mutter.

stretch: to reach out or extend

> I had to stretch to get the glass from the cabinet's top shelf.

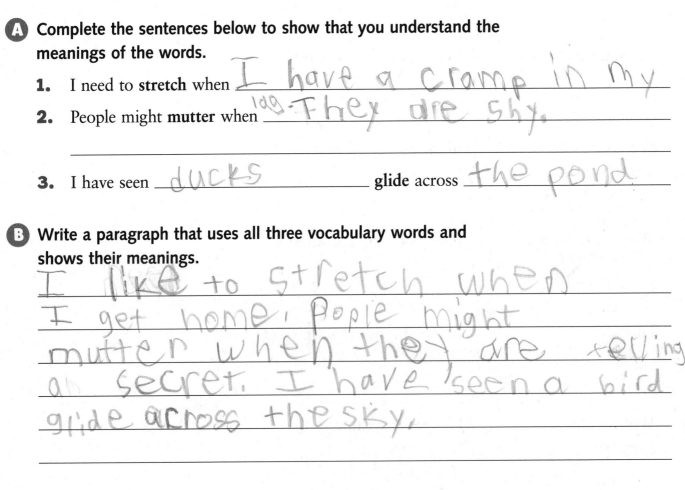

A Complete the sentences below to show that you understand the meanings of the words.

1. I need to **stretch** when _I have a cramp in my leg._

2. People might **mutter** when _They are shy._

_____

3. I have seen _ducks_ **glide** across _the pond_

B Write a paragraph that uses all three vocabulary words and shows their meanings.

I like to stretch when I get home. Pople might mutter when they are telling an secret. I have seen a bird glide across the sky.

_____

_____

Make Connections

Read about the vocabulary words. Follow the directions to complete the activities.

stretch

When something is stretched, it is spread out to its full length.

1. List three things that **stretch**. legs, pony holder, sweater

You might hear someone say, "That's a stretch!" This exclamation means that what has been described is hard to believe. Think about it as "stretching the truth."

2. What other phrase could you use instead of "That's a stretch"? That's not true.

mutter

The word *mutter* is often used to describe the way people talk when they are angry but do not want their anger to show. When you mutter, your mouth hardly moves. How might other parts of your body look if you were angry and muttering? Circle the words or phrases that you think fit.

3. eyes (in slits) crying wide open (looking away) glowing

4. hands (clenched) relaxed in fists clapping pointing

5. shoulders tight slumped crooked (hunched) upright

glide

A gliding motion is smooth and easy. You cannot glide over a bumpy surface.

6. List three surfaces that are smooth enough for something to glide across.
Ice, water, snow

7. Choose one surface you have listed above and describe something gliding across it.
penguin on ice

Prefixes *un-*, *dis-*, and *mis-*

			Frequently misspelled words	Review words
dislike	unload	mislead		
unplanned	uncover	misjudge	while	manage
misplace	disorder	uneven	during	notice
discolor	untrue	untidy		
unpaid	displease			
distrust	mistreated			

A **Choose the spelling word that best completes each sentence below.**

1. I really enjoy eating broccoli, but I _____ spinach.

2. Sarah's room is always neat, but her brother Bobby's is _____.

3. I rarely _____ my keys, but today I can't find them anywhere!

4. Once we _____ these groceries, we can pack the trunk with our camping gear.

5. My hairdresser usually cuts my hair pretty straight, but this time my bangs are _____.

6. Anna always pays her bills on time, so I was surprised to learn that her overdue library fines were still _____.

7. If you add bleach to those bright clothes, you will _____ the fabric.

B **Read the paragraph. On the lines below, rewrite the paragraph and correct any errors in spelling, capitalization, and punctuation.**

Henry's mother was displeesed by the dissorder in his untidie bedroom. he seemed to mipslace a lot of his things because his room was so messy His mother dislicked it so much that she told him his allowance would go unpayed until he cleaned it up. while he was cleaning, he uncoverred a book that he had lost last year. He felt bad because he had misjudjed his little sister when he accused her of taking it He went to her room and told her he was sorry for disstrusting her and mistreeting her. his sister knew that his accusations were untru and was happy that he realized he had been mislede. To make it up to her, henry agreed to unlode the dishwasher for the rest of the month He also kept his room clean from that day forward

_____

_____

_____

_____

_____

_____

_____

_____

_____

Letter

Practice reading this letter to a partner.

Letter from the Prairie

October 5, 1910

My dear Grandmother,

I hope this finds you well, and I'm sorry for not writing sooner. We have been so very busy with our new life in Nebraska. Our days are filled with farming and tending to the animals. I never knew a person could be so tired at the end of the day!

I scarcely know where to begin to tell you about our new life. Our work starts before dawn casts its light over the edge of the fields. I complete my first task, feeding the animals, before breakfast. Then I help Mama in the house while Papa and the boys tend to the crops. The next day it begins all over again.

At first I missed the city terribly. Lately, though, wherever I look, I see the majestic beauty of the land. The best part is how the sky stretches out forever. I wonder if I'll ever get used to that.

I hope that you can visit us soon. You would love it here. It is so peaceful and so lovely!

Love,

Josephine

Did you read the letter with fluency? Use the form on the next page to evaluate yourself and your partner.

Reading Response Form

A On a scale of 1 to 5, rate yourself and your partner. Do this for the first reading and final readings, at least. On a scale of 1 to 5, 5 is considered outstanding, 3 is good, and 1 is average.

1. Did I …

	First Reading	Second Reading	Final Reading
Read the words correctly?			
Read at a good pace?			
Read with expression?			
Read clearly for my audience?			

2. Did my partner …

	First Reading	Second Reading	Final Reading
Read the words correctly?			
Read at a good pace?			
Read with expression?			
Read clearly for the audience?			

B After the first reading, share with your partner how you thought he or she read, and offer suggestions for improvement.

C After the final reading, answer the following questions for yourself.

1. What did I do well?

First Reading _____

Second Reading _____

Final Reading _____

2. What should I do to improve my reading next time?

First Reading _____

Second Reading _____

Final Reading _____

Make Predictions

When you **make predictions** about a text, you:

- Make thoughtful guesses before you read about what might happen

- Use clues from the text and pictures

- Use what you have read to predict what will happen next

Before you read a text, you should make reasonable guesses about its content.

Continue to make predictions as you read. You might predict what will happen next or how information will fit together.

Make Predictions

Confirm and revise predictions as you read. As you learn more information, it can affect your original predictions or prove them to be correct.

Remember that you are the most important part of any prediction that you make. Trust yourself, what you already know about the subject, and the text itself and you will make good predictions.

Read the information about each book. Use text and photo clues as well as prior knowledge to make a prediction about the book.

Title: *Family Reunion*

Cover Art:

Description on Back Cover:

Sean O'Brien grew up in New York City. But now he's headed for a family reunion in Iowa. What fun adventures could possibly await him on his uncle's farm?

My Prediction	Clues	What I Know
I predict Sean's trip will be …		

Title: *One Tree, Please*

Cover Art:

Description on Back Cover:

Kirsten loves trees. But in the barren plains of North Dakota, there just aren't many to be found. For her 12th birthday, Kirsten has just one wish: a climbing tree in her yard. Will her wish come true?

My Prediction	Clues	What I Know
I predict Kirsten's wish …		

Similes

> **Similes** compare two unlike things. Similes:
>
> - Use the word *like* or *as* to signal the comparison
>
> - Help readers picture what is being described
>
> - Relate unfamiliar things to familiar things

In a simile, the word *like* or *as* joins the two things being compared. Similes help you understand how something looks, feels, moves, or acts.

Similes That Use *like*	Similes That Use *as*
The barge eased through the canal *like* a knife slicing through warm butter.	The river shimmered *as* if jewels were beneath the water.
Because the wind was so strong, the seagulls had to walk sideways *like* crabs.	As a result of the drought, the ground was dry *as* a lizard's skin.

Similes also can help you figure out the meanings of words that you do not know. In similes, those words are compared to something you might know. Look at the examples from the sentences above.

- You could understand the meaning of *eased* by picturing how simple it is to cut through warm butter.

- You could understand the meaning of *shimmered* by thinking of words that describe jewels, such as *sparkle, glitter, shine,* and so on.

- The meaning of *sideways* becomes clearer when you think about how crabs move.

- The sentence lets you know that *drought* is connected to "dry ground," but the image of the lizard's skin helps you understand that *drought* has to do with severe dryness and lack of rain.

A Complete these sentences. Choose words that will help people picture what is being described.

1. The pillow was as soft as _____

2. The man's kind words were like _____

3. His heart pounded like _____

4. The wind howled as if _____

5. Spring smelled sweet like _____

B Follow the directions in order to write your own similes.

1. Make a list of things that have curves. _____

_____

Write a simile that could help someone picture a very curvy road. _____

_____

2. Make a list of things that move very quickly. _____

_____

Write a simile to help someone see a person running at top speed. _____

_____

3. Make a list of things that are smooth. _____

_____

Write a simile that could help someone picture a smooth lake. _____

_____

Before and After Reading

Circle the number that matches how you feel about each statement. "1" means you absolutely agree. "5" means you neither agree nor disagree. "10" means that you totally disagree with the statement.

Statement	Agree ⟵⟶ Disagree
1. Parenting is one of the toughest jobs there is.	1 2 3 4 5 6 7 8 9 10
2. Children should work to pay for the things they want.	1 2 3 4 5 6 7 8 9 10
3. You can really only become friends with people who are a lot like you.	1 2 3 4 5 6 7 8 9 10
4. Children can teach adults how to do some things.	1 2 3 4 5 6 7 8 9 10
5. It is difficult to have fun in places with really cold weather.	1 2 3 4 5 6 7 8 9 10
6. Real communication can only happen when there is a shared language.	1 2 3 4 5 6 7 8 9 10
7. It is impolite to refuse food that you do not like or cannot eat.	1 2 3 4 5 6 7 8 9 10
8. Nothing is as scary as what you can imagine.	1 2 3 4 5 6 7 8 9 10
9. Children should be given adult responsibilities.	1 2 3 4 5 6 7 8 9 10
10. You can learn a lot from people in a short amount of time.	1 2 3 4 5 6 7 8 9 10

Mood and Tone

Mood is the feeling you get from reading a story.

Tone is how the author feels about a story.

Read the following passage and then answer the questions below.

Katie could not believe the day had finally arrived. She and thousands of other New Yorkers were watching as Governor DeWitt Clinton led a parade of four boats into New York Bay. The boats had come all the way from Lake Erie in just nine days! After eight years of construction, the Erie Canal was finally open.

Katie lifted her small son so he could see the boats. As the boats approached, cannons and fireworks lit up the sky, making a great noise. Everyone cheered, including Katie. As the governor poured the water he had brought all the way from Lake Erie into the bay, Katie felt proud to be a part of such a historic moment. She kissed her son and whispered, "Just wait. Soon everyone will know that we live in one of the greatest cities in the world!"

1. What is the mood of the passage? How do you know? _____

_____

_____

_____

2. How do you think the author feels about what is described in this passage? _____

_____

_____

_____

Read and Respond

Read the questions. Write your answers on the lines.

1. *Marven of the Great North Woods* is based on a true event. If you were going to write a story about something that has happened in your life, what event would you choose? Write a brief description of this event.

   _____

   _____

   _____

2. Marven showed plenty of courage in this story. If you were able to write to Marven about his courage, what would you say? Be sure to give examples from the story.

   _____

   _____

   _____

3. Marven remembered things that he had learned from other people as he tried to deal with his situation. What is an important lesson you have learned from someone in your life? Be sure to tell who taught you the lesson.

   _____

   _____

   _____

4. Would you like to be in the place and time of this story? Why or why not?

   _____

   _____

   _____

Identify Cause and Effect

When you read, you will often find cause-and-effect relationships. These relationships are often signaled by words such as *so* and *because*.

A **cause** is *why* something happens.	→ An **effect** is *what* happens as a result of a cause.

Look at this excerpt from page 263 of *A Tour of the Central Region* and the student notes below it. Then answer the questions.

The Saint Lawrence Seaway allows goods grown or made in the Midwest to be transported, or sent, to the rest of the world. Cities such as Chicago, Illinois, and Cleveland, Ohio, benefit because of shipping on the Great Lakes.

The St. Lawrence Seaway has many ports.	Goods can be shipped to many places.	Midwestern cities sell many goods and make money.

1. What is one effect of sea ports? _____

2. Why do cities such as Chicago and Cleveland benefit from sea ports? _____

_____

3. What signal word can you find in the paragraph? _____

Prefixes That Tell *Where*

Some prefixes describe where something is. The box below lists examples of prefixes that describe *where*.

Prefix	Meaning	Example
ex-	out	**export**: to ship or send out
a-	on	**across**: on the other side
mid-	in the middle	**Midwest**: the middle region of the U.S.
re-	again or back	**reverse**: to move back
trans-	across	**transport**: to ship or send across

A Combine the roots with the prefixes and suffixes below. Write the new word and tell what it means. The first one has been done for you.

1. ex + it = *exit: to leave a place*

2. mid + town = _____

3. re + emerge = _____

4. trans + continental = _____

5. a + blaze = _____

B Write a sentence each for two of the words in Activity A.

1. _____

_____

2. _____

_____

Inquiry Checklist: Week 3

Put a check mark next to each item once it is complete.

Share New Information

☐ Each person in my group shared information.

☐ We revised our conjecture if our understandings changed.

☐ We filled in the Idea Tracker for Week 3.

---

6. Develop Presentation

☐ We chose a format for our presentation.
    PRACTICE COMPANION 16, 373

☐ We talked about how we might use technology in our presentation.

☐ We created the presentation format.

☐ We used the Presentation Organizer to plan our presentation.

☐ We gave a speaking part to each group member.

☐ All group members completed their Week 3 Inquiry Planners.
PRACTICE COMPANION 62

Notes:

_____

_____

_____

_____

_____

_____

_____

_____

Inquiry Planner: Week 3

Write your group's updated Inquiry Question and conjecture. Then write your Action Plan for next week.

My group's updated Inquiry Question is: _____

_____

My group's updated conjecture is: _____

_____

Action Plan

1. What topics will I collect information for?_____

_____

_____

2. What sources will I use? _____

_____

_____

3. Where will I find these sources? _____

_____

_____

4. When will I collect information? _____

_____

_____

5. How will I record the information? _____

_____

_____

Focus Question: What is life like in the Midwest?

List some features of how life in the Midwest in the past was different from life there today. Fill in the chart with answers from your selection.

Past	Today

What makes the Midwest special? Use examples from your selection to explain your answer.

_____

_____

_____

_____

_____

_____

_____

_____

Focus Question: What is life like in the South Central States?

The South Central States include Texas, Oklahoma, Louisiana, Arkansas, Mississippi, Kentucky, Tennessee, and Alabama. What do you know about these states? What might life be like in the South Central States? Write your answers in the chart below.

State	Things I Know
Texas	
Oklahoma	
Louisiana	
Arkansas	
Mississippi	
Kentucky	
Tennessee	
Alabama	

My Weekly Planner

Week of _____

Theme Vocabulary	This week's words:
Differentiated Vocabulary	This week's words:
Comprehension Strategy and Skill	This week's comprehension strategy: This week's comprehension skill:
Vocabulary Strategy	This week's vocabulary strategy:
Spelling/Word Study Skill	This week's spelling skill:
Word Study Skill	This week's word study skill:
Fluency	This week's fluency selection:
Writing and Language Arts	This week's writing form:
Grammar	This week's grammar skills:

Writing with Vocabulary Words

A Choose two words from the vocabulary list. Then use both words in a sentence. Use every word at least once. You will use one word twice. If you need to, you can add word endings to the word.

basin	flourish	mutter
delta	glide	stretch
diverse	landform	transport

1. _____
   _____

2. _____
   _____

3. _____
   _____

4. _____
   _____

5. _____
   _____

B Use at least four of the words from the word bank above to write a paragraph that answers the Unit Theme Question *What makes the Central Region special?*

_____
_____
_____
_____
_____

Synonyms and Examples

The words in the box below are either synonyms or examples of each vocabulary word. Write each word from the box next to the vocabulary word that it goes with.

carry	grumble	skate
deliver	lengthen	slide
desert	mountain	thrive
different	plateau	triangle
extend	sink	varied

1. basin _____

2. delta _____

3. diverse _____

4. flourish _____

5. glide _____

6. landform _____

7. mutter _____

8. stretch _____

9. transport _____

Suffixes -*ful*, -*less*, -*ness*, and -*ment*

			Frequently misspelled words	Review words
fondness	useless	endless		
treatment	statement	neatness		misplace
cheerful	movement	speechless	tonight	dislike
restless	truthful	peaceful		
colorful	beautiful		someone	
weakness	clumsiness			

A Sort the spelling words based on the meanings of their suffixes.

"full of"
Cheerful
Colorful
truthful
beautiful
peaceful

"without"
restless
useless
endless
speechless

Suffix Meanings

"quality of"
fondness
weakness
clumsiness
neatness

"act of, result of"
treatment
statement
movement

B Choose one of the spelling words to complete each analogy below.

1. light : dark :: strength : _____

2. smart : intelligent :: happy : _____

3. parrot : _____ :: dove : white

4. _____ : awake :: exhausted : asleep

5. tiny : huge :: chatty : _____

C Proofread the paragraph. Circle the misspelled words, and then write them correctly on the lines below.

Trudy had always had a fundness for beautyful sunsets. Whenever she felt restles, she would go outside at dusk and enjoy the colorfull, peeceful beauty of the sunset. It was a weackness of hers and it always left her speachless. The movment of the sun into the endles sky made her calm and thoughtful. Somone once told her that watching the sunset was usless and silly and couldn't really make her feel more chearful. She knew that statement was not troothful and continued to enjoy the sunsets whenever she could.

1. _____

2. _____

3. _____

4. _____

5. _____

6. _____

7. _____

8. _____

9. _____

10. _____

11. _____

12. _____

13. _____

Journal Entry

Practice reading this journal entry to a partner.

Life in Louisiana

Dear Journal,

It was another scorcher in New Orleans today! I think the temperature went past 90 degrees, and I can't even tell you how bad the humidity is this time of year. Amos and I went swimming today to try to beat the heat. It was really refreshing, but it only took a few minutes out of the river before I started sweating again. Thank goodness it's supposed to rain tomorrow. Hopefully that will cool things off a bit.

The hot weather doesn't seem to bother Dad. He's been really busy on the boat this spring. He's caught so many shrimp! That's always good news for our family since I can eat shrimp all day, every day!

I can't wait 'til I'm old enough to work on the boat with Dad. I'll be a fourth generation fisher. It makes me proud just to think about it.

Leroy

Did you read the journal entry with fluency? Use the form on the next page to evaluate yourself and your partner.

Reading Response Form

A On a scale of 1 to 5, rate yourself and your partner. Do this for the first reading and final readings, at least. On a scale of 1 to 5, 5 is considered outstanding, 3 is good, and 1 is average.

1. Did I ...

	First Reading	Second Reading	Final Reading
Read the words correctly?			
Read at a good pace?			
Read with expression?			
Read clearly for my audience?			

2. Did my partner ...

	First Reading	Second Reading	Final Reading
Read the words correctly?			
Read at a good pace?			
Read with expression?			
Read clearly for the audience?			

B After the first reading, share with your partner how you thought he or she read, and offer suggestions for improvement.

C After the final reading, answer the following questions for yourself.

1. What did I do well?

First Reading _____

Second Reading _____

Final Reading _____

2. What should I do to improve my reading next time?

First Reading _____

Second Reading _____

Final Reading _____

Determine Important Information

Experienced readers make note of the ways in which writers present important information.

Determine Important Information
You determine important information by figuring out the ideas the author wants you to remember.

Writers often use visual aids to explain important information. If you read about something in the text and then see it presented in a chart or map as well, that information is probably important.	The amount of text a writer uses to present certain information helps you figure out what is most important.	When you read fiction, remember that information about story elements is also important to notice. These elements include main characters, setting, plot, and conflict.
Ask yourself: Why is this visual aid on the page? What should I learn from it?	**Ask yourself:** What's most important on this page? Why is it so important? How much space did the writer use to tell me this information?	**Ask yourself:** What important information did I learn about (name of character) / (setting) / (story problem) here?

Read the passage below. Think about which information is most important.

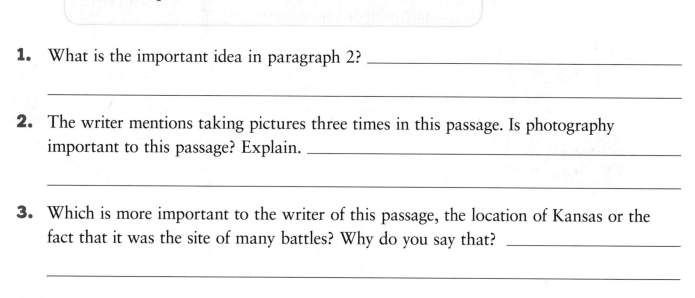

Before Alaska and Hawaii became states, Kansas was the geographical center of the United States. Near the town of Lebanon, you can visit a stone monument that marks the exact center of the first 48 states. Many people have their pictures taken here.

Horse lovers like to be photographed beside a different type of monument—a stuffed horse named Comanche. Comanche was the only survivor of Custer's Last Stand. After this famous battle, he was found badly wounded, standing over his master's body. Once Comanche healed from his injuries, he was given special treatment for the rest of his life. When he died, Comanche was prepared for permanent display at a museum in Lawrence.

There are many other places to have your picture taken in Kansas. A famous log cabin, several forts, and a Pony Express station are just a few examples.

1. What is the important idea in paragraph 2? _____

_____

2. The writer mentions taking pictures three times in this passage. Is photography important to this passage? Explain. _____

_____

3. Which is more important to the writer of this passage, the location of Kansas or the fact that it was the site of many battles? Why do you say that? _____

_____

_____

Use Multiple Strategies

Antonyms

Antonyms are words with opposite meanings. To be antonyms, words must be the same part of speech.

day/night
quickly/slowly
funny/serious
stop/start

Thesaurus

You can find antonyms as well as synonyms for words in a thesaurus.

cold: cool, chilly, frigid, bleak, bitter

hot: warm, baking, sunny, tropical, thermal

Similes

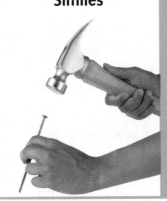

Similes show comparisons between two different things. Similes use the word *like* or *as* to signal the comparison.

The hail struck the roof as hard as a hammer hitting a nail. The day was moving like molasses.

A Answer the question below.

1. Alex is trying to think of an antonym for *unhappy*. Where can he get help? _____

_____

B The listed words are synonyms for *happy*. Think of an antonym for each word. Do not use any word twice. Use a thesaurus if you need help. The first one has been done for you.

1. happy— *unhappy*_____

2. glad—_____

3. pleased—_____

4. joyful—_____

5. content—_____

C Write an antonym for the boldfaced word in the sentence. Remember that antonyms must be the same part of speech.

1. The movie seemed very **short,** but the advertisements for future movies seemed _____.

2. I was **hungry** this morning, but after finishing a stack of pancakes I was _____.

3. Have you ever seen a **tame** fox, or are they always _____ animals?

4. Some people work at their jobs all **night** and then sleep all _____.

D Write two sentences that contain similes to compare unlike things.

1. _____

_____

2. _____

_____

Before and After Reading

Before you read the next selection, answer True or False to the following statements. Review the statements again after reading to see if your answers have changed.

Before reading	The Music Makers	
	Statement	**After reading**
	1. Music can bring people together.	
	2. Main characters stay the same from the beginning to the end of a story.	
	3. Different regions of the country often have music that is special to that region.	
	4. The title of this story hints that the story is about musicians.	
	5. A story set in New Orleans will be about hurricanes.	

Before reading	The Flute Player and the Rabbit	
	Statement	**After reading**
	1. Folktales often include story elements that could not happen in real life.	
	2. The characters in a folktale often have special powers.	
	3. Folktales can teach lessons about life.	
	4. The setting of a story does not affect what happens in the story.	
	5. People are often rewarded for helping others.	

Racing for Land

Before reading	Statement	After reading
	1. Stories teach us more about the present than the past.	
	2. The characters in a story often face a challenge.	
	3. The land in this country was not occupied by anyone before the settlers arrived.	
	4. Stories about the past often include real facts about the past.	
	5. Family stories teach us about our families' pasts.	

Delta Blues

Before reading	Statement	After reading
	1. Music inspires people and comforts them during difficult times.	
	2. The characters in a play are always from the present time.	
	3. Plays are more difficult to understand than stories.	
	4. Musical talent often passes from one generation to another in families.	
	5. The blues is a form of music that expresses sadness but also hope for better times.	

Identify Cause and Effect

The **cause** is why something happens, and the **effect** is what happens
as result of the cause.

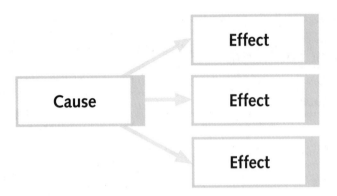

A Read the excerpt below from page 281 of *A Tour of the Central
Region*. Then complete the chart.

The civil rights movement quickly spread all over the country.
As a result, laws were passed that guaranteed equal voting and
property ownership rights.

Cause	Effect

B Now read page 284 in *A Tour of the Central Region*. Then provide
an effect for each cause listed below.

1. The land in the Central Region is good for farming.

_____

2. There are many waterways in the Central Region.

_____

3. The Central Region has good soil, waterways, and great resources.

_____

4. People brought their traditions with them to the Central Region.

_____

Greek and Latin Roots

Many words in the English language have **Greek and Latin roots.**
Some common Greek and Latin roots are listed below.

Roots	Meanings
phon	voice or sound
photo	light
mot	move
spec and *vid*	look or see
sign	mark or sign
graph	write

A **Combine the parts of the word and write the new word on the line. The first one has been done for you.**

1. tele + phone = _telephone_

2. sign + al = _____

3. tele + graph = _____

4. mot + ive = _____

5. photo + graph = _____

B **Write a definition for each of the words in Activity A.**

1. _____

2. _____

3. _____

4. _____

5. _____

C **Write a sentence that uses a word containing a *vid* or *spec* root.**

_____

Inquiry Checklist: Week 4

Put a check mark next to each item once it is complete.

Discussion Roles

☐ Each person in my group shared information.

☐ We revised our conjecture if our understandings changed.

7. Deliver Presentation

☐ We rehearsed our presentation.

☐ We presented for another group.

☐ We used the Presentation Rubric to evaluate our own presentation.

☐ We used the Presentation Rubric to evaluate the other group's presentation.

☐ We received feedback. We used the Presentation Organizer to revise our presentation.

Identify New Questions

☐ All group members listed new questions on their Week 4 Inquiry Planners.

PRACTICE COMPANION **81**

☐ We posted new questions on the Question Board.

Notes:

_____

_____

_____

_____

_____

_____

_____

_____

Inquiry Planner: Week 4

Write your new questions and your plans for finding out more.

1. What other questions do I have? _____

_____

_____

2. What sources can I use to find out more? _____

_____

_____

3. Where will I find these sources? _____

_____

_____

4. When will I collect information? _____

_____

_____

Self-Assessment Rubric

Read each goal in the chart. Make a check mark to give yourself a
score of 3, 2, or 1. Then complete the sentences below.

Category	Goals	Very Good 3	OK 2	Needs Work 1
Group Role	I understood my role. I did the job and helped my group.			
Participation	I helped my group complete each step of the Inquiry Process.			
Research	I did research on my own. I shared it with my group.			
Listening	I gave others a chance to speak and listened well.			
Collaboration	I shared my ideas and respected others' ideas.			
Responsibility	I stayed on task during group work.			
Presentation	I was prepared for our presentation and I spoke clearly.			
Enjoyment	I enjoyed working with others in my group.			

1. One thing I did well was _____

_____

2. One thing I would like to improve is _____

_____

Focus Question: What is life like in the South Central States?

What was life like in the South Central States in the past? What is it like today? Use your selection to fill in the box below.

Past	Present

What makes the Central Region special? Use examples from your selection to explain your answer.

_____

_____

_____

_____

_____

_____

Study the Model

Biography

Read the Writing Model along with your teacher. Look for the strong adjectives and the order of the events.

The Adventures of Mark Twain

by Sean Byrne

"I have never let my schooling interfere with my education." These are the famous, clever, and funny words of one of America's best writers, Mark Twain. But did you know that Mark Twain was not the real name of the American writer? His real name was Samuel Langhorne Clemens. Born in 1835, he grew up in Missouri. His experiences growing up near the mighty Mississippi River would influence his writing in the years to come.

Clemens first began writing for a newspaper. There he started using the pen name Mark Twain. Clemens based that name on his boating experiences, the word *twain* meaning "twelve feet deep." After years of being a journalist, Twain started writing books.

In two of his most famous novels, Twain drew from his experiences of living near the longest river in the United States. His novel *The Adventures of Tom Sawyer* is about a boy who runs away on the Mississippi River. Twain based the book on what happened to people he knew—even himself! A later well-known novel by Twain is *The Adventures of Huckleberry Finn*. In this book, people talk the same way that people in Missouri did at the time. Dialogue that is written the way people speak is called *colloquial*. Twain popularized this style, and it forever changed the way American writers wrote books. Readers could better relate to the characters in Twain's books because they could "hear" the voices of the characters on the page.

In the spring of 1910, Samuel Clemens, or Mark Twain, died of a heart attack. Although the "father of American literature" passed away, he has remained one of the most famous American writers of all time and continues to influence both writers and readers alike.

Evaluation Rubric

Biography

Category	Goals	Yes	Needs Work!	Now it's OK.
Organization	The biography tells the events in the person's life in the correct order.			
	I include an introduction, middle paragraphs, and a conclusion.			
Ideas	The biography tells about important events in the person's life.			
	I give examples that show why this person is interesting.			
Voice	The writing sounds like my writing.			
Word Choice	I use strong adjectives to clearly describe the person.			
Sentence Fluency	I use sequence words to explain the order of the events in the person's life.			
	My information flows smoothly from one sentence and paragraph to the next.			
Conventions	I use capital letters at the beginning of each sentence and for all proper nouns.			
	I use correct punctuation, including using commas with multiple adjectives.			
	All the words are spelled correctly.			
	I have corrected any errors in grammar.			

Biography

Peer Review

Read your partner's paper. Then finish each sentence.

1. I see that this biography is organized with _____

_____

_____

_____

2. Some strong adjectives that the author uses to describe the person are _____

_____

_____

_____

3. Some sequence words that the author might use are _____

_____

_____

_____

Name of Reader _____

Descriptive Adjectives

Adjectives that describe *what kind, which one,* and *how many* can make your writing more interesting and keep your readers engaged.

Look at the example below. Note how the descriptive adjectives enhance the sentence.

Example:

The flowers grew.

With Descriptive Adjectives:

The multitude of fragrant flowers grew tall and strong.

Look at the words below. Write a sentence that uses the noun and descriptive adjective correctly. The first one has been done for you.

1. book/interesting

The interesting book held my attention all day.

2. dog/friendly

_____

3. movie/scary

_____

4. car/new

_____

5. meal/spicy

_____

6. horn/blaring

_____

7. surface/smooth

_____

8. coat/tattered

_____

Adjectives That Compare

Comparative adjectives compare two things, and superlative adjectives compare three or more things. Use *-er* and *-est* to compare with single-syllable adjectives.

Comparative Adjectives *-er*

- This cup is <u>larger</u> than that cup.

- My tie is <u>shinier</u> than the tie on display.

Superlative Adjectives *-est*

- This is the <u>largest</u> cup in the cupboard.

- This tie is the <u>shiniest</u> tie on the shelves.

Look at the words below. Use *-er* and *-est* to write two sentences that use both of the words. The first one has been done for you.

1. dress/new

The cotton dress is newer than the silk dress.

This dress is my newest dress.

2. house/old

_____

_____

3. book/thick

_____

_____

4. train/loud

_____

_____

More/Most and *Better/Best*

When an adjective has more than one syllable, you will usually use *more* to form the comparative and *most* to form the superlative.

Eliza is more comfortable playing the piano than Harry.

Some adjectives have irregular comparative and superlative forms, such as *good/better/best*. These adjectives do not use *-er* and *-est* or *more* and *most*.

Sasha is a good speller, but Eli is the best speller in class.

A Complete each sentence by writing the correct form of the adjective in parentheses. The first one has been done for you.

1. My mother makes the _best_ spaghetti in the world! (good)

2. I like fish _____ than chicken. (good)

3. My new room is _____ than my old room. (large)

4. These are the _____ cherries I have ever tasted. (sweet)

5. His directions to the party are _____ than the directions I got online. (complicated)

6. Sandra wrote the _____ essay in the whole class. (organized)

7. A quilt is _____ than a sheet. (thick)

8. What is the _____ color in the world? (popular)

B Write two sentences that each use a comparative adjective.

1. _____

2. _____

Use Commas in a Series

When you use adjectives in your writing, be sure to look carefully at the punctuation in your sentences. Use commas between adjectives when three or more adjectives are used in a series. Look at the information in the boxes for "commas with adjectives" guidelines.

Use a comma if the adjectives give similar kinds of information.

- What a long, thin, and flat fish!

- It was a bright, sunny day.

Do not use a comma if adjectives give different kinds of information.

- Hand me the small white pillow.

- I have a fat striped cat.

Decide if the sentences below are written correctly. Write "Correct" or "Incorrect" on the lines. The first one has been done for you.

1. She is a kind friendly neighbor. _Incorrect_____

   She is a kind, friendly neighbor. _Correct_____

2. Kris wore a beautiful new hat. _____

   Kris wore a beautiful, new hat. _____

3. Fernando is a patient considerate boy. _____

   Fernando is a patient, considerate boy. _____

4. I swim in a clear cool and crisp lake. _____

   I swim in a clear, cool, and crisp lake. _____

5. This is an exciting, and interesting story. _____

   This is an exciting and interesting story. _____

6. Dan has a fast new car. _____

   Dan has a fast, new car. _____

7. It was a soft light and calming song. _____

   It was a soft, light, and calming song. _____

Using Test-Taking Strategies

Sometimes, instead of choosing an answer to a test question or prompt, you must plan and write your own answer. Here is a sample question based on *Marven of the Great North Woods*.

Sample Question:

> **Describe how Marven feels when he first enters the logging camp.**

> Look carefully at what the question asks you to do.
>
> - You must infer how Marven feels.
>
> - You must provide details to support, or explain, your inference.
>
> There are different ways to answer this question. Here are some possible answers:
>
> - Marven feels delighted. On page 286, it says that Marven hears "the lively squeaks of a fiddle" and it seems "the horses are keeping time to the music." On this page, Mr. Murray teases Marven because he can tell he likes the music.
>
> - Marven feels shocked. You know this because the text states that he has never seen men as large as the lumberjacks.
>
> - Marven feels curious. You know this because he wants to keep watching the lumberjacks.

When you write your own answer, pay attention to what the question asks. Then plan a response that meets the expectations of the question or prompt.

Applying Test-Taking Strategies

Read the prompt below and identify what is needed for a response.

The story *Marven of the Great North Woods* is historical fiction. Choose three details about the setting, characters, or events and tell why they are realistic. Then tell why they were important parts of the story.

Use information from *Marven of the Great North Woods* to complete the chart and plan your response. One idea is given.

Detail from *Marven of the Great North Woods*	Why It Is Realistic	Why It Is Important
Many lumberjacks do not speak English.	French Canadian lumberjacks worked in logging camps.	Marven makes friends with lumberjacks despite language differences.

Use the ideas in the chart to write your response to the prompt at the top of the page. Write your response on a separate sheet of paper. Make sure you include everything the prompt requires.

My Weekly Planner

Week of _____

Theme Vocabulary	This week's words:
Differentiated Vocabulary	This week's words:
Comprehension Strategy and Skill	This week's comprehension strategy: This week's comprehension skill:
Vocabulary Strategy	This week's vocabulary strategy:
Spelling/Word Study Skill	This week's spelling skill:
Word Study Skill	This week's word study skill:
Fluency	This week's fluency selection:
Writing and Language Arts	This week's writing form:
Grammar	This week's grammar skill:

Identify Examples

When learning words that identify big concepts, think of *examples* that will help you to understand the meaning of the words.

Interdependence is when two or more people or things depend on, or need, each other. Look at the sentence below.

> **To live and to make milk, cows need grass to eat. For grass to grow, there must be good soil, sun and rain.**

Cows need grass, and the grass needs soil. The two are *interdependent*.

Read the words in the box. Choose three words that are examples of the theme vocabulary words listed below the box. Write the examples in the blanks under the correct vocabulary word.

rain forest	disease
thorns	desert
fur	claws
pond	classroom

1. **survive:** to remain alive (Hint: Think about what might be used to help living things stay alive.)

   _____

   _____

   _____

2. **ecosystem:** the living and nonliving things that interact within a community (Hint: Think about places where things are interdependent.)

   _____

   _____

   _____

Write Sentences

A Write one sentence for each of the theme vocabulary words. The meaning of each vocabulary word should be clear in the sentence.

1. _____

2. _____

3. _____

B Match each word below to one of the numbered theme vocabulary words. Then use each matched pair in sentences to show how the words are connected.

- **camouflage:** coloring that makes living things blend into their environment
- **decomposers:** animals that break down dead things so the nutrients can feed the soil
- **habitat:** the place where a plant or animal naturally lives and grows

1. interdependence/_____

_____

_____

_____

2. survive/_____

_____

_____

_____

3. ecosystem/_____

_____

_____

_____

Words with VCCV Pattern

lumber	canyon	engine	**Frequently misspelled words**	**Review words**
plastic	fortune	collect		colorful
support	effort	seldom	anyway	weakness
attend	perfect	picture	coming	
traffic	danger			
survive	soccer			

A Look at this week's spelling words. Write the word, and then draw a line between the syllables in each word. The first one is done for you.

1. l u m b e r   _lum|ber_
2. p l a s t i c   _____
3. s u p p o r t   _____
4. a t t e n d   _____
5. t r a f f i c   _____
6. s u r v i v e   _____
7. c a n y o n   _____
8. f o r t u n e   _____
9. e f f o r t   _____
10. p e r f e c t   _____
11. d a n g e r   _____
12. s o c c e r   _____
13. e n g i n e   _____
14. c o l l e c t   _____
15. s e l d o m   _____
16. p i c t u r e   _____

B Proofread the paragraph. Circle the misspelled words and write them correctly on the lines below.

The trafic on the way to our soccar game this morning was less than perfekt. A truck carrying some lombar had slipped on some ice as it was comming around a corner and logs were all over the road. Luckily, the truck didn't swerve into the caynon so there was no immediate dangre. It was going to take quite the efort to get all of the logs off the road and keep the cars moving. The police were there to attand to the cleanup and to help colect the logs. It was quite a pitcure. All we could do was listen to our idling engin and hope that it would all get cleaned up soon. Fortunately, the fire department came to suport the police and there was soon a lane open for cars to pass. We were on our way to the game at last!

1. _____

2. _____

3. _____

4. _____

5. _____

6. _____

7. _____

8. _____

9. _____

10. _____

11. _____

12. _____

13. _____

Feature Article

Practice reading this feature article to a partner.

The Jewels of the Forest

by Sam Rockwood

Have you ever taken a jaunt through a scenic forest? What an amazing way to spend an afternoon! Imagine this: tall trees sway in the breeze. The cheerful music of melodic birds tickles your ears. Animals rustle through the brush. And if you're lucky, you spot a deer.

The forest is a constant flurry of activity, even when it appears peaceful and quiet. The sun, shining brightly on the plants, urges them to grow and flower. The rain, pouring down, soaks the soil, and thirsty roots reach for its moisture.

Deer amble through the forest, searching for food, their ears raised, listening for predators. Squirrels hurriedly dig for nuts while birds patiently construct their intricate nests, twig by twig.

The next time you stroll through the forest, take it all in. Breathe in the fresh air and sunshine, or feel the light rain on your face. Marvel at the way all parts of the forest fit together, like jewels in a necklace, for all to enjoy.

Did you read the feature article with fluency? Use the form on the next page to evaluate yourself and your partner.

Reading Response Form

A On a scale of 1 to 5, rate yourself and your partner. Do this for the first reading and final readings, at least. On a scale of 1 to 5, 5 is considered outstanding, 3 is good, and 1 is average.

1. Did I ...

	First Reading	Second Reading	Final Reading
Read the words correctly?			
Read at a good pace?			
Read with expression?			
Read clearly for my audience?			

2. Did my partner ...

	First Reading	Second Reading	Final Reading
Read the words correctly?			
Read at a good pace?			
Read with expression?			
Read clearly for my audience?			

B After the first reading, share with your partner how you thought he or she read, and offer suggestions for improvement.

C After the final reading, answer the following questions for yourself.

1. What did I do well?

First Reading _____

Second Reading _____

Final Reading _____

2. What should I do to improve my reading next time?

First Reading _____

Second Reading _____

Final Reading _____

Make Inferences

Making inferences helps you fill in gaps that the author has left in a text. To make inferences, you use clues from the text and add them to what you already know to help you understand the text.

| Clues in text | **+** | What I know | **=** | Inference |

The example below shows how text information combined with what you know can lead you to make inferences.

My Backyard

My backyard is an ecosystem that works like a bicycle. It has many parts that all fit together. For one thing, we have a lot of raspberries, and we put up a fence to keep the rabbits out of them. Birds also like to eat the berries, and so do we. A pump from our basement drains water into a small pond. It waters the raspberry patch. Birds of all kinds like the pond too.

What I read	What I know	Inference
Just like a bicycle, an ecosystem has different parts that need one another to work. Each separate part is important to the whole ecosystem.	Every spring, we plant flowers and plants in our garden. Rabbits and insects eat plants for food.	My garden is an important part of the ecosystem where I live because it helps other living things survive.

Use the example on the previous page to help you complete the chart below. The text for the first column of the chart has been provided for you.

Remember that …

Clues in text	**+**	What I know	**=**	Inference

What I read	What I know	Inference
Ecosystems are nature's communities. They exist everywhere in the world.		
All ecosystems need space, even if it is under a rock. This space is called a habitat.		
Each part of an ecosystem does a certain job. Each job helps living things meet their basic needs, such as finding food and shelter.		

101

Connotation and Denotation

As you know, you use a dictionary to look up the meanings of words. Some words, particularly those that describe us and our surroundings, often contain more meanings than just their dictionary definitions.

- **Denotation** is the actual meaning of a word.

- **Connotation** refers to the feeling a word might give you.

The word *home* has both denotation and connotation. Denotation describes the dictionary definition of the word *home*.

home (hōm) *n.* the place where a person lives; My home is in the city.

What do you feel when you think about the word *home*? Many people hear the word *home* and think of family, fun, food, comfort, laughter, and closeness. These thoughts are the *connotations,* or the feelings, that the word *home* gives them.

Choose one word from the box below and write a simple dictionary definition, or denotation, for that word in the top box. Then fill in the other spaces with words that show connotations of the word you chose.

consumer	desert	nonliving
North Pole	predator	swamp
ocean		

Categorize and Classify

Recall that **categorizing** and **classifying** mean putting things together into groups to better understand how they are related.

A Look at a student's notes about the unit *Nature's Neighborhoods.* Then answer the questions.

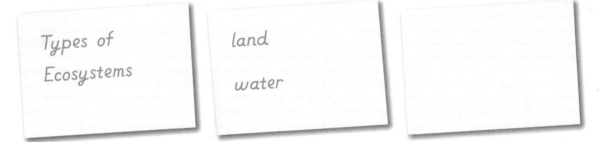

Types of Ecosystems

land

water

1. What is the category? _____

2. What information can you add to a third note?

_____

B Read this paragraph and then answer the questions.

> Herbivores, carnivores, and omnivores are types of consumers. Carnivores and omnivores are predators. They hunt and eat other animals. The animals they hunt are called prey. A predator can also be the prey for a larger predator. For example, a lizard hunts insects, but some birds hunt lizards. Top predators, such as mountain lions, are not prey.

1. How would you categorize the terms *herbivores, carnivores,* and *omnivores?* _____

2. What is an example of an animal that is only a predator?

_____

3. What animal can be classified as both predator and prey?

_____

Latin and Greek Roots

- The root *act* means "to do": active (moving about)

- The root *bio* means "life" and the root *ology* means "science of": bio + ology = biology (science of life)

- The root *cycle* means "circle or ring": bicycle (vehicle with two wheels)

A **Read the words in the box. Circle the root or roots found in each word.**

actor	cyclist
unicycle	reaction
bioactive	biome

B **Using your knowledge of Latin and Greek roots, write the word from the box that matches each definition below.**

1. a vehicle with one wheel _____

2. a person who performs _____

3. a response to an activity _____

4. a habitat that supports life _____

5. a person in a bike race _____

6. affecting living things _____

Inquiry Checklist: Week 1

Put a check mark next to each item once it is complete.

Discussion Roles

☐ I took a role in my group.

PRACTICE COMPANION **370**

My role is _____.

---

1. Generate Ideas and Questions

☐ We thought of at least three possible questions.

☐ We chose an Inquiry Question to investigate.

---

2. Make a Conjecture

☐ We shared what we know about our Inquiry Question.

☐ We made a conjecture about our Inquiry Question.

☐ We filled in the Idea Tracker for Week 1.

☐ We posted our Inquiry Question and conjecture on the Question Board.

---

3. Make Plans to Collect Information

☐ We made a list of topics to research and split them up among the group.

☐ We used the Information Finder and made a list of possible sources to use. PRACTICE COMPANION **371**

☐ All group members completed their Week 1 Inquiry Planners.
PRACTICE COMPANION **107**

Notes:

_____

_____

_____

_____

Inquiry Planner: Week 1

**Write your group's Inquiry Question and conjecture. Then write
your Action Plan for next week.**

My group's Inquiry Question is: _____

_____

My group's conjecture is: _____

_____

Action Plan

1. What topics will I collect information for?_____

_____

_____

2. What sources will I use? _____

_____

_____

3. Where will I find these sources? _____

_____

_____

4. When will I collect information? _____

_____

_____

5. How will I record the information? _____

_____

_____

Diagram

Read about diagrams and study the example.

What Is a Diagram?

- A diagram is a drawing or series of drawings that explain an idea, a process, or how something works.

- It sometimes includes words as labels or descriptions.

- It may include arrows to show the order things happen.

- It has a title.

Diagram of a Lever

You Can Use Technology

Find out how technology can help you create and share your presentation.

- Log on to **www.wgLead21.com**.

- From My Home Page, click on Inquiry Project.

Focus Question: What roles do the parts of an ecosystem play?

What living and nonliving things are found in the ecosystem you read about? What roles do these things play in the ecosystem? Fill in the chart with your answers.

Living Things	Roles in Ecosystem
Nonliving Things	Roles in Ecosystem

How are living things connected? Use examples from your selection to explain your answer.

_____

_____

_____

_____

_____

_____

Focus Question: Why do living things need each other?

Think about the following living things: *birds, plants,* and *caterpillars.* Why might they need each other? Write your answers on the lines below.

   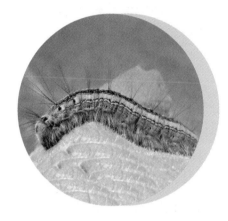

Plants and Birds _____

_____

_____

_____

Plants and Caterpillars _____

_____

_____

_____

Birds and Caterpillars _____

_____

_____

_____

My Weekly Planner

Week of _____

Theme Vocabulary	This week's words:
Differentiated Vocabulary	This week's words:
Comprehension Strategy and Skill	This week's comprehension strategy: This week's comprehension skill:
Vocabulary Strategy	This week's vocabulary strategy:
Spelling/Word Study Skill	This week's spelling skill:
Word Study Skill	This week's word study skill:
Fluency	This week's fluency selection:
Writing and Language Arts	This week's writing form:
Grammar	This week's grammar skill:

Complete Ideas

A Read about Latin words and roots in the explanations below. Match each word from the box with the correct explanation.

affect	disappear	compete

1. This word is from *com* (meaning "together") and *petere* (meaning "to rush out"). The English word is defined as "to be in a state of rivalry or to win or gain something."

_____

2. This word is from *facere* (meaning "to do" or "to make"). The English word is defined as "to influence or change."

_____

3. This word is from *parere* (meaning "to come forth") and *dis* (meaning "the opposite of"). The English word is defined as "to pass from view or to stop existing."

_____

B Complete the sentences below.

1. Teams who **compete** against each other are _____.

2. If something **disappears,** you can no longer _____.

3. You only **affect** a thing if you _____ it.

Related Words

A Circle the word in each row that best relates to each vocabulary
word. The first one has been done for you.

Vocabulary Word	Choose the Best Related Word	
1. compete	(race)	chase
2. affect	teach	change
3. disappear	hide	vanish
4. eventually	soon	finally
5. adaptations	vary	agree
6. behavior	action	conduct

B Write a sentence that tells how the word you circled goes
with the vocabulary word. Use both the vocabulary word and
its related word in your sentence. You may change the form of
the word if you wish. One has been done for you.

1. *Many runners competed in our annual street race last year.*

2. _____

3. _____

4. _____

5. _____

6. _____

Words with VCV Pattern

			Frequently misspelled words	Review words
event	planet	polite		collect
lemon	student	punish		
humor	detail	moment	because	support
habit	unite	protest	thought	
rapid	frozen			
recess	figure			

A Find and circle this week's spelling words in the word snakes below. Then fill in the missing letters on that word in the word list and draw a line to separate the syllables. The first one is done for you.

z e v e n t w r q s t u d e n t c r

p l a n e t x l e m o n z

z h s f   p u n i s h v

t y p r o t e s t d g   m o m e n t h

z s s e   o r e c e s s

u n i t e y u h a b i t w r a p i d   d e t a i l z

z s f r o z e n v   h p o l i t e x

b f i g u r e b   t h u m o r f h

1. e | v e n t
2. s t _ _ e n t
3. _ l a n e _
4. l e _ o n
5. p r _ t e s t
6. p u _ _ s h
7. m _ m e n t
8. _ n i t e

9. h a _ _ i t
10. _ _ p i d
11. r e c e _ _
12. _ e t a i l
13. f r _ z e n
14. f i g _ _ _
15. p o _ i t e
16. h u m _ _

B **Proofread the paragraph. Circle the spelling words that are misspelled and write them on the lines below. Underline any spelling words that are spelled correctly.**

"Students," Mrs. Florian said, "we are going to take part in a special event right now." The class was surprised becus this time was normally reces time and was seldom used for anything else. At that momment, though, an interesting figur walked into the classroom, wearing a suit with many fun detales on it. He was a magician! The man gave the class a polite bow and with a rapid wave of his hands, he pulled a bright, yellow lemmon out of thin air! The class was frozin in amazement and then they unitted in applause. It was the magician's habit to tell jokes as he performed his tricks, and the class all thout he had a great sense of humer. When he was finished the class protested and wanted to see more. But that was all the time that the magician had.

1. _____   6. _____

2. _____   7. _____

3. _____   8. _____

4. _____   9. _____

5. _____   10. _____

Realistic Fiction

Practice reading this realistic fiction selection to a partner.

The Hidden Hunter

by Felicity Greggs

The tall grass that matched her fur so well camouflaged the lioness. She watched the zebra slowly edge closer to her hiding place in the brush. Preparing to pounce, the lion reared onto her back paws. Just as she was about to leap forward, the zebra startled and, in an instant, fled.

The lion had been hunting for hours but had nothing to show for it. She was built to be a great hunter: sleek, silent, with superior senses to detect nearby prey. But now she was hot, she was weary, and she was disheartened. What would she bring back to the pride?

The lion sulked, dejected and hungry. Suddenly she raised her head and sniffed the air. A gazelle! She raced silently through the grasses and leapt toward the gazelle. The elegant animal bounded away, but the speed and strength of the lion was too great. Her powerful front legs brought the gazelle to the ground. Today, her pride would not go hungry.

Did you read the realistic fiction selection with fluency? Use the form on the next page to evaluate yourself and your partner.

Reading Response Form

A On a scale of 1 to 5, rate yourself and your partner. Do this for the first reading and final readings, at least. On a scale of 1 to 5, 5 is considered outstanding, 3 is good, and 1 is average.

1. Did I …

	First Reading	Second Reading	Final Reading
Read the words correctly?			
Read at a good pace?			
Read with expression?			
Read clearly for my audience?			

2. Did my partner …

	First Reading	Second Reading	Final Reading
Read the words correctly?			
Read at a good pace?			
Read with expression?			
Read clearly for my audience?			

B After the first reading, share with your partner how you thought he or she read, and offer suggestions for improvement.

C After the final reading, answer the following questions for yourself.

1. What did I do well?

First Reading _____

Second Reading _____

Final Reading _____

2. What should I do to improve my reading next time?

First Reading _____

Second Reading _____

Final Reading _____

Summarize

When you **summarize,** you:

- Use your own words to tell about the text briefly

- Share the most important ideas about the text

- Arrange the ideas so they connect well together

Read the paragraphs and a student's summary of them that follows.

People are often surprised to learn that Antarctica gets more sunlight in a year than countries on the equator. However, the heat from all of that sunlight does not warm up Antarctica because much of the sunlight is reflected away by the bright white snow.

Because of the cold, howling winds and freezing temperatures, Antarctica is difficult for human life. For this reason, scientists who study the area live at work stations only during certain times of the year.

However, not all life finds Antarctica too harsh. Many animals thrive in the seas around Antarctica where there is an abundance of tiny shrimp-like animals known as krill. Whales, fish, seals, birds, and other animals feed on krill and keep the ecosystem thriving.

Even though Antarctica gets plenty of sunlight, this sunlight does not warm up this frozen place. The only humans who brave the freezing temperatures are scientists studying the area. However, there is plenty of animal life found in the rich ecosystem in the waters around Antarctica.

A Read each passage. Then write a sentence that summarizes each passage. The first one is done for you.

> The Arctic tundra are treeless plains covered by snow and ice much of the year. During a very short summer, the temperature is only about 15 degrees above freezing.

Cold, treeless plains known as the tundra are found in the Arctic.

> Few plants can live in the tundra. Shrubs, grasses, and mosses survive because they live close to the ground. Tundra plants grow just as soon as the snow melts, and the short summer begins.

_____

> Most tundra animals also appear just for the summer. Caribou travel many miles to reach the tundra. Birds also make the long trip. Only musk oxen survive well in the tundra throughout the year.

_____

B Create a summary using your answers from Part A.

_____

_____

_____

_____

Idioms

An **idiom** is an expression common to a particular culture that does not mean what it literally says. Its meaning is different from the usual meanings of the individual words. You have to learn the meanings of idioms, just like you learn the meanings of words.

> For many Americans, the expression "play it by ear" means "to do something without planning." But in England, a piano player might respond by saying, "I'd rather have the actual music."

Read the following. See if you can guess what each idiom means.

Sometimes you can find hints by reading around the idiom. Look at the words leading up to the underlined idiom.

> **Mia was very tired. She got into bed, turned off the light, and <u>called it a day</u>.**

Sometimes an idiom can be found in a dictionary under its main word. The main word in this idiom is *thumb*.

> **"I am <u>all thumbs</u> today," she said with a sigh.**

Sometimes you just have to ask for the meaning of an idiom.

> **I got <u>cold feet</u> when it was time to perform in the play.**

A Read the idiom on the left and fill in what you think it means on the right. The first one has been done for you.

music to my ears	*something that sounds pleasant*
keep your eyes peeled	
she was all smiles	
nose for news	
stiff upper lip	
face the music	
keep your chin up	

B Circle the main word in each idiom. Think about that word's meaning to help you understand the idiom.

1. got the axe

2. burned the candle at both ends

3. hit the roof

4. kept a straight face

5. was on cloud nine

C Complete the sentences with one idiom from Activity B.

1. That joke was so funny! I don't know how you
_____ while telling it.

2. Hank _____ all week.
That is why he is still asleep at noon.

3. The coach _____ today.
He was let go with five games left in the season.

4. I lent my friend my best shirt. She got stains all over it. I
_____ when she told me it
was ruined.

5. I _____ when I got my
new bike!

Categorize and Classify

Categorize	Classify
Explains how parts of a group are alike	Group things with similar features into the same category

A Read the paragraph. Then use the organizer to classify information that belongs in the category "A Camel's Creature Features."

Camels have many "creature features" that help them adapt to life in the desert. Two rows of long, thick eyelashes keep sand out of their eyes. Their humps store fat, so they can go without food and water for a long time. Thick pads on the bottoms of their hooves allow them to walk in the hot, coarse sand.

A Camel's Creature Features

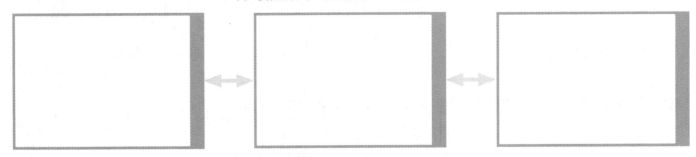

B Reread pages 342–345 in *Nature's Neighborhoods*. Use the organizer to classify species in the category "Invasive Species."

Invasive Species

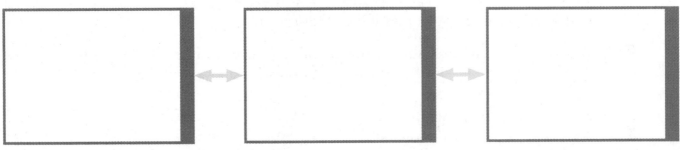

Comparatives and Superlatives

The suffixes -er and -est are added to many adjectives to make the comparative and superlative forms of a word. Sometimes adding the suffix can change the spelling of the word.

tall + er = taller

tall + est = tallest

I am taller than Jan.

Alicia is the tallest girl in school.

tiny + er = tinier

tiny + est = tiniest

This flower is tinier than that one, but yours is the tiniest plant of all.

A **Combine the adjectives with the suffixes -er or -est. The first one has been done for you.**

1. shallow + est = *shallowest*

2. mild + est = _____

3. ugly + er = _____

4. bare + est = _____

5. calm + est = _____

B **Write the form of the adjective that fits the description.**

1. her most fancy dress _____

2. more old than Scott _____

3. the most cheap fare to Utah _____

4. a house's most grand room _____

5. more strong than Trudy _____

Inquiry Checklist: Week 2

Put a check mark next to each item once it is complete.

Collect Information

☐ I used the Evaluating Sources Checklist to check my sources.

PRACTICE COMPANION **372**

☐ I recorded information from at least one good source using an Investigation Sheet.

4. Organize and Synthesize Information

☐ Each person in my group shared information.

☐ We organized the information using the Chain Organizer or another type of organizer.

☐ We synthesized the information and found at least one new idea.

5. Confirm or Revise Your Conjecture

☐ We used our new understandings to decide if we should revise our conjecture or our Inquiry Question.

☐ We filled in the Idea Tracker for Week 2.

☐ We posted our revised Inquiry Question and conjecture on the Question Board.

☐ All group members completed their Week 2 Inquiry Planners.

PRACTICE COMPANION **125**

Notes:

_____

_____

_____

_____

_____

Inquiry Planner: Week 2

Write your group's updated Inquiry Question and conjecture. Then write your Action Plan for next week.

My group's updated Inquiry Question is: _____

_____

My group's updated conjecture is: _____

_____

Action Plan

1. What topics will I collect information for? _____

_____

_____

2. What sources will I use? _____

_____

_____

3. Where will I find these sources? _____

_____

_____

4. When will I collect information? _____

_____

_____

5. How will I record the information? _____

_____

_____

Think Back
Selection 2

Focus Question: Why do living things need each other?

What animals and plants did you read about? In the chart below, explain how these living things need each other.

Plants	Animals	How They Need Each Other

How are living things connected? Use examples from your selection to explain your answer on the lines below.

_____

_____

_____

_____

_____

_____

Focus Question: What happens when there are changes to an ecosystem?

Think about the following events: *pollution, flood,* and *children cleaning up a park*. How might each of these change an ecosystem? Write your answers on the lines below.

Pollution might _____

_____

_____

A flood might _____

_____

_____

Children cleaning up a park might _____

_____

_____

Study the Model

Science Report

Read the Writing Model along with your teacher. Look for descriptive words and accurate scientific details.

Poison Dart Frogs: Friend and Foe

by Jason Ancic

In the hot, humid tropical rain forests of Central and South America, poison dart frogs live exotic lives. With their bright colors and their powerful venom, these stunning animals are both friend and foe to humans. Some species are endangered.

The smallest species of poison dart frogs is less than 1.5 centimeters. That's smaller than the size of a paper clip! Although they are small animals, poison dart frogs are hard to miss. What the frogs lack in size, they make up for with bright, brilliant colors and patterns. Poison dart frogs can be blue, purple, green, red, yellow, or orange. One might think that this bright coloring would attract predators, but it actually warns them to stay away.

Poison dart frogs are among the most toxic animals on Earth. One species has enough venom to kill 10 grown men! Scientists aren't sure where the poison comes from, but they think the frogs take in plant poisons from the ants, termites, and beetles they eat.

The poison is dangerous, but it can be helpful too. For hundreds of years, people who live in the rain forest have put the poison in the tips of blowgun darts for hunting. The poison could be used for medicines too. Scientists are learning that a venom that usually causes pain might actually be able to be used as a painkiller!

Some people may say that endangered poison dart frogs are not worth saving, because they are dangerous. We need to remember, however, that they also can help us. Who knows what other endangered species that could be a help to humans are still undiscovered?

Evaluation Rubric

Science Report

Writing Traits	Goals	Yes	Needs Work!	Now it's OK.
Organization	My report has an introduction, a body, and a conclusion. I only include information that belongs with the topic.			
Ideas	Each paragraph has a main idea and interesting supporting details. My facts are accurate.			
Voice	My writing sounds interesting.			
Word Choice	I used interesting words to clearly describe my topic.			
Sentence Fluency	I used a variety of sentence types. My writing sounds like a science report when read aloud.			
Conventions	I used capital letters at the beginning of each sentence and for all proper nouns. I used correct punctuation. All the words are spelled correctly. I use adjectives and adverbs correctly.			

Science Report

Peer Review

Read your partner's paper. Then finish each sentence.

1. I see that this report is organized by _____

   _____

   _____

   _____

2. Some scientific facts the author uses are _____

   _____

   _____

   _____

3. Some supporting details that the author might want to include are _____

   _____

   _____

   _____

Name of Reader _____

Comparing with Adjectives

The words *good, better, best,* and *many, more,* and *most* are used before **adjectives** that do not take the comparative endings *-er* and *-est.* When you write, make sure that you use comparative and superlative adjectives correctly.

Todd attends a *good* cooking school.

Mary attends a *better* cooking school than Todd.

Manny attends the *best* cooking school of all.

Del worked *many* years.

Don has worked *more* years than I have.

Lu has worked the *most* years of all of us.

Choose the word that best completes each sentence. The first one has been done for you.

1. That is the (better, best) tasting cookie I have ever had.
   best

2. Dad has played that song (many, more) times.
   many

3. He wants a (good, better) spelling grade on his next quiz than on his last one. _better_

4. Camping is (many, more) fun than fishing.
   more

5. Who is the (better, best) diving member on the team?
   best

6. She is wearing the (more, most) beautiful dress I have ever seen.
   most

7. That is the (good, best) behaving dog in the show!
   best

8. Who is the (more, most) interesting person you have ever met?
   most

Commas in a Series

When you write, make sure you use **commas** correctly with adjectives in a series. If you have more than one adjective describing a noun, put a comma between them. Do not put a comma between the last adjective and the noun.

> There rose a dark threatening and low-hanging cloud.
>
> There rose a dark, threatening, and low-hanging cloud.

Read the following sentences. Write "Correct" if commas are used correctly. If commas are not used properly, write the corrected sentence on the line provided. The first one has been done for you.

1. She is a kind helpful and generous teacher.

   She is a kind, helpful, and generous teacher.

2. She wore very bright and colorful gloves.

   _____

3. He is a clever intelligent and quick learner.

   _____

4. I like to swim in the deep, cool, blue, and clear ocean.

   _____

5. I just saw an interesting and funny movie.

   _____

6. Mike likes ice cream with red blue and green sprinkles.

   _____

7. Cary gave the most stunning elegant and moving speech.

   _____

8. The pickle left a bitter sour taste in my mouth.

   _____

Adverbs That Tell *How*

When **adverbs** modify verbs, they can tell how, or the way in which something happens. Adverbs that tell how usually end in *-ly*. Adverbs do not always follow directly after the verbs they modify.

Carefully, Ann cleans up the broken glass.

The adverb *carefully* modifies the verb *cleans*. It tells how Ann cleans.

The family works well together.

The adverb *well* modifies the verb *works*. It tells how the family works.

A **Read the sentences. Write the adverb and the verb it modifies. The first one has been done for you.**

1. Jim learns quickly.

   quickly, learns

2. The dog begs constantly during dinner time.

   _____

3. Tina stood on the stage and gratefully accepted her award.

   _____

4. Patiently, Hugo waited for the bus.

   _____

5. The duck plunged suddenly into the water.

   _____

B **Write a sentence using each of the adverbs from activity A. The first one has been done for you.**

1. _Mom says she always walks quickly past the candy store._

2. _____

3. _____

4. _____

5. _____

Adverbs That Tell *When* and *Where*

When adverbs modify verbs, they can tell when or where an action happens. Recall that adverbs do not always follow directly after the verbs they modify.

> Trang: When will we eat lunch?
>
> Cam: We will eat soon.
>
> Trang: Where do you like to eat?
>
> Cam: I eat there on Tuesdays.
>
> - The adverb *soon* tells when. It modifies the verb *eat*.
>
> - The adverb *there* tells where. It modifies the verb *eat*.

A **Read the sentences. Write the adverb and the verb it modifies. The first one has been done for you.**

1. The grocery store is nearby. *nearby, is* _____

2. The children are playing outside. _____

3. Kathy finished her work early. _____

4. I always send my grandmother a card on her birthday.

   _____

5. My Aunt Marion moved far away. _____

B **Write a sentence using each of the adverbs from Part A. Then identify if the adverb tells "when" or "where" an action happens. The first one has been done for you.**

1. *I go to the school that is nearby. (where)* _____

2. _____

3. _____

4. _____

5. _____

Using Test-Taking Strategies

Read this sample question based on Chapter 1 of *Balance in the Wild.*

Which is true of all ecosystems?

(A) They take up a great deal of space.
(B) They have more living things than nonliving things.
(C) They stay the same no matter what the weather is like.
(D) They are made up of many important parts.

Use the text to eliminate answer choices:

- Is (A) a possible answer? No, because page 320 says that some ecosystems are "so tiny that they fit under a rock."

- Is (B) a possible answer? Look at page 321. It says that all ecosystems have living and nonliving things, but it says nothing about there being more living than nonliving things.

- Is (C) a possible answer? Look at the second paragraph on page 321. It says an ecosystem can be changed by its climate. If weather changes over time, climate change can result and this can change an ecosystem.

- Is (D) a possible answer? Look at the first paragraph on page 322, which says that everything in an ecosystem is important.

By thinking carefully about each answer choice, and checking back to see what the story says, you can pick the correct answer. In this case, D is the answer.

Applying Test-Taking Strategies

Here are more questions to answer. Look carefully at each answer choice. Cross off the letter of any choice you know is wrong.

1. The author uses the example of a bicycle to show

   Ⓐ how parts of an ecosystem depend on each other.
   Ⓑ that nonliving things are important to ecosystems.
   Ⓒ why ecosystems are more alike than different.
   Ⓓ how ecosystems develop over time.
   (page 322)

2. How do decomposers help an ecosystem?

   Ⓐ By recycling bottles and papers into new material
   Ⓑ By changing bacteria and fungi into nonliving things
   Ⓒ By breaking down nonliving things into parts of soil
   Ⓓ By creating all the food scavengers need to consume
   (pages 334–335)

3. What is an example of an adaptation that helps an animal survive?

   Ⓐ A mule deer's place in the food chain
   Ⓑ A mountain goat's split hooves and thick coat
   Ⓒ An earthworm eating dead plants and animals
   Ⓓ A black bear climbing a tree to escape danger
   (pages 336–337)

4. Which of these can be a danger to an ecosystem?

   Ⓐ Making homes from recycled wood
   Ⓑ Having predators at the top of the food chain
   Ⓒ Bringing in species from another ecosystem
   Ⓓ Having more producers than consumers
   (pages 338–345)

My Weekly Planner	
Week of _____	
Theme Vocabulary	This week's words:
Differentiated Vocabulary	This week's words:
Comprehension Strategy and Skill	This week's comprehension strategy: This week's comprehension skill:
Vocabulary Strategy	This week's vocabulary strategy:
Spelling/Word Study Skill	This week's spelling skill:
Word Study Skill	This week's word study skill:
Fluency	This week's fluency selection:
Writing and Language Arts	This week's writing form:
Grammar	This week's grammar skill:

Roots and Meanings

A Read about the roots of the words in the chart below. Then look up the word in your glossary and fill in the meaning. The first one has been done for you.

Word	Root	Root Meaning	Word Meaning
fragrant (p. 372)	bhrag	to smell	*having a pleasant smell*
plodding (p. 366)	plod	the sound of plodding	
hesitated (p. 376)	ghais	to be stuck	

B Write complete sentences using the directions below.

1. Use the word *fragrant* to describe something you might find in a garden.

_____

_____

2. Use the word *plod* to describe what you might experience crossing a muddy field.

_____

_____

3. Use the word *hesitate* to explain what you might do to safely cross a busy street.

_____

_____

_____

_____

Related Words

Each of the words in the box below is related to one of the vocabulary words. Write the word in the rectangle below its related vocabulary word. Then add more examples of related words to fill the rectangles.

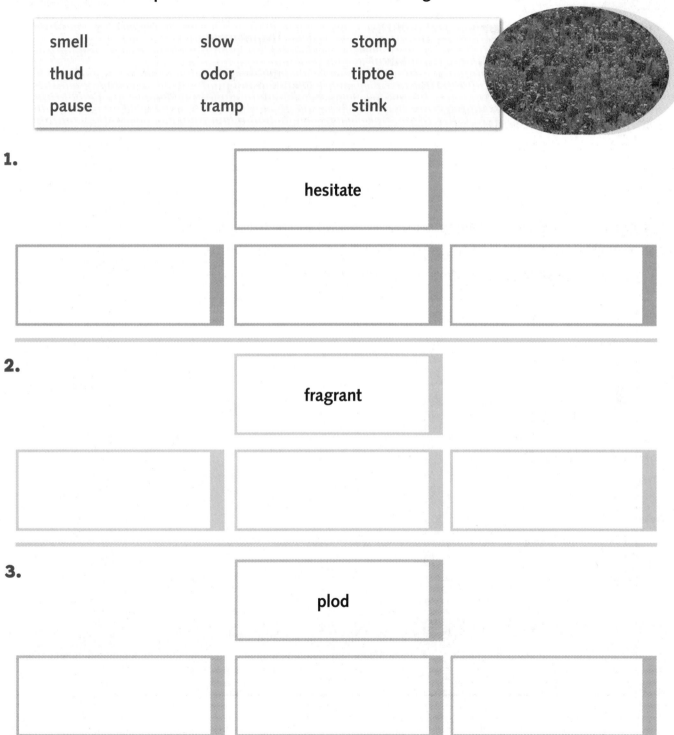

smell	slow	stomp
thud	odor	tiptoe
pause	tramp	stink

1.

hesitate

2.

fragrant

3.

plod

Words with VCCV and VCV Patterns

			Frequently misspelled words	Review words
capture	shelter	diner		
narrow	recent	famous		frozen
reward	broken	finish	tomorrow	detail
dentist	dinner	silver	goodbye	
hollow	ahead			
corner	divide			

A Look at this week's spelling words. Find and circle these words in the Word Search below. Hint: some letters are used in two words. The first one, *capture*, has been done for you.

C	O	R	N	E	R	A	H	E	A	D	S
D	A	D	N	A	R	R	O	W	S	F	G
I	K	P	O	G	E	X	L	S	L	A	T
V	Q	D	T	R	W	R	L	H	F	M	A
I	W	I	S	U	A	E	O	E	I	O	E
D	I	N	N	E	R	C	W	L	N	U	P
E	Y	E	U	G	D	E	N	T	I	S	T
P	B	R	O	K	E	N	H	E	S	W	E
S	I	L	V	E	R	T	E	R	H	E	R

B **Proofread the paragraph. On the lines below, rewrite the paragraph, correcting any errors in spelling, punctuation, or capitalization.**

after his most resent trip to the dentest, oliver was heading home for diner when he saw something silvre lying on the ground He thought it might be a piece of silverware from the dinner on the corner, but it was a necklace. the clasp was brocken, but it was still beautiful He took the necklace to the police station, which was just up ahed. he found out that it belonged to one of the most famos singers on the planit. The necklace had been stolen, but the police had been unable to captur the thief The singer was offering a rewrd to whoever found the necklace. oliver finnished filling out some paperwork, and the police told him that he would have the reward by tommorow. He said goodby to the police officers and went home to decide how to divid up his reward amongst his family members

Poem

Practice reading this poem to a partner.

After Wind and Rain

by Henry Callahan

The rain fell for two days straight
While the wind blew water all around.
And when it finally settled down,
A new world emerged, looking drowned.
After they came, the wind and the rain,
The hurricane over, but the damage done.
And the animals that survived the storm
Knew their problems had just begun.
After they came, the wind and the rain,
The habitats of many disappeared.
Some animals died, and some ran away,
But those that survived persevered.
After they came, the wind and the rain,
The land and the sea strived to improve.
But everything had changed so much
That many found they had to move.
A hurricane is a dangerous storm,
Damaging everything in its way.
Its wind, its rain, affect every life form,
And the roles that each one plays.

Did you read the poem with fluency? Use the form on the next page to evaluate yourself and your partner.

Reading Response Form

A On a scale of 1 to 5, rate yourself and your partner. Do this for the first reading and final readings, at least. On a scale of 1 to 5, 5 is considered outstanding, 3 is good, and 1 is average.

1. Did I ...

	First Reading	Second Reading	Final Reading
Read the words correctly?			
Read at a good pace?			
Read with expression?			
Read clearly for my audience?			

2. Did my partner ...

	First Reading	Second Reading	Final Reading
Read the words correctly?			
Read at a good pace?			
Read with expression?			
Read clearly for my audience?			

B After the first reading, share with your partner how you thought he or she read, and offer suggestions for improvement.

C After the final reading, answer the following questions for yourself.

1. What did I do well?

First Reading _____

Second Reading _____

Final Reading _____

2. What should I do to improve my reading next time?

First Reading _____

Second Reading _____

Final Reading _____

Make Connections

When you **make connections** while reading, you relate the text to:

Your own knowledge

Information from other texts

Issues and ideas in the world

Shannon is doing research for a report on plants. She is reading about how plants defend themselves.

> Plants have enemies. Many animals eat them. Disease attacks them. Even nature harms plants with things like fire and frost. But plants have ways of defending themselves.
>
> Some plants have structures that protect them. Thorns and other prickles are examples. Animals do not like to be stuck! Thick bark is another example. Insects, cold, and heat cannot get through these structures very easily.

Make your own connections as you read about plant defenses. Does the passage remind you of something that has a connection to you? Does it remind you of something else you have read? Does it relate to something in the world as a whole?

Fill in the chart and check the circle that describes what you have written. Check Self, Text, or World. The first one has been done for you.

From the text
Some plants make poisons. These poisons can cause animals who eat the plant to get sick.

This reminds me of
I read that plants have enemies and that plants have ways of defending themselves.

Connection
○ Self
● Text
○ World

From the text
Some plant poisons cause trouble when the plant is touched. Poison oak and poison ivy are examples.

This reminds me of

Connection
○ Self
○ Text
○ World

From the text
Some of the poisons and other compounds found in plants can be made into medicines to treat cancer and other diseases.

This reminds me of

Connection
○ Self
○ Text
○ World

Shades of Meaning

There can be slight differences in meaning between similar words and phrases. Think about the shades of meaning that related words have and choose the word that best fits your purpose.

- Think about the words *pleased* and *joyful*. Each word relates to feeling "happy." However, *joyful* has a shade of meaning that best describes someone who is very happy.

- Connotation is another important thing to think about when choosing between related words. A person who gets an unexpected bill will be more *shocked* than *surprised* at the amount he or she has to pay.

- Think about a snake making its way across a yard. An author who writes that the snake "*slithered* through the grass" would give a clearer description of that act than an author who writes that the snake "*moved* through the grass."

Now look at the table below. Read each word in the first column. Then read the related words that have different shades of meaning than the provided word.

look	stare	peek	study	glare
touch	pinch	grab	scrape	scratch
talk	murmur	shout	converse	argue

Complete each sentence below by choosing the related word in the parentheses that best fits the sentence. The first one has been done for you.

1. Anne (raced, strolled) to the platform to catch the train before it left.

raced

2. The plate fell to the floor and (broke, shattered) into many little pieces.

_____

3. The field was (damp, flooded) after three days of rain.

_____

4. The bird (took, snatched) the cracker from my hand when I was not looking.

_____

5. I (flipped, flung) the ball with all my might.

_____

6. The (feast, meal) he prepared was made up of soup and salad.

_____

7. The harsh winds (slammed, closed) all the doors in the house.

_____

8. The scientists (met, discovered) more examples of Native American pottery at the site.

_____

9. Heather was (hungry, starving) after missing breakfast.

_____

10. They (entered, invaded) the movie theater and took their seats.

_____

Before and After Reading

Circle the number that matches how you feel about each statement. "10" means you totally disagree. "5" means that you neither agree nor disagree. "1" means that you absolutely agree with the statement.

Statement	Agree ⟵⟶ Disagree
1. Rain forests are important to the whole world.	1 2 3 4 5 6 7 8 9 10
2. People should think about how their actions affect nature.	1 2 3 4 5 6 7 8 9 10
3. All living things have a role in the world.	1 2 3 4 5 6 7 8 9 10
4. Forests are more beautiful than other places.	1 2 3 4 5 6 7 8 9 10
5. Beauty is more important than money.	1 2 3 4 5 6 7 8 9 10
6. People sometimes do not realize when they are rude to others.	1 2 3 4 5 6 7 8 9 10
7. Some plants and animals cannot live anywhere except the rain forest.	1 2 3 4 5 6 7 8 9 10
8. Providing places for people to live is more important than protecting animal habitats.	1 2 3 4 5 6 7 8 9 10
9. The most important value of a tree is how much wood, nuts, and fruit it can produce.	1 2 3 4 5 6 7 8 9 10
10. Most places in the world would never change if it were not for people.	1 2 3 4 5 6 7 8 9 10

How Characters Change

Characters in stories can change, just as people change in real life. One way to understand how and why characters change is to think about the sequence of facts and events in the story.

Before you read *The Great Kapok Tree*, read and think about the information in the sequence chart below. What does the chart tell you? After you read the story, write the answers to the questions in the middle boxes of the chart. The first one has been done for you.

First, we meet the two men. As they walked into the forest,

> "all was quiet as the creatures watched the two men and wondered why they had come."

What did the smaller man want to do?

He wanted to cut down the great Kapok tree.

What was the problem with cutting down the tree?

_____

What did the animals do when the man fell asleep?

_____

What did the man do when he awakened?

_____

How did the man change by the end of the story?

_____
_____
_____

Read and Respond

Read the questions. Write your answers on the lines.

1. Think about what the animals whispered into the man's ear. What would you tell the man to make him change his mind about chopping down the kapok tree?

_____

_____

_____

2. What do you believe the man was thinking as he was about to swing his axe at the tree for the last time? How did his thoughts change?

_____

_____

_____

3. What was your favorite part of the story? Why?

_____

_____

_____

4. Think of a place in the world that you would like to see stay the same. What would you tell someone about this place if that person wanted to change it?

_____

_____

_____

5. Look back at the sequence of events in the chart on page 149. Write a description about how the man's character changed in *The Great Kapok Tree*.

_____

_____

_____

Compare and Contrast

When you **compare**, you tell how two things are alike.
When you **contrast**, you tell how two things are different.

A Venn diagram is a useful tool for comparing and contrasting two different things.

A Use the chart below to compare and contrast bees and boa constrictors. Then answer the questions that follow.

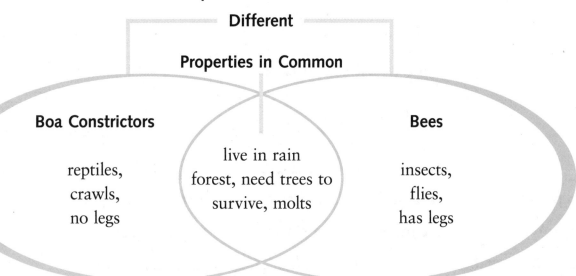

Different

Properties in Common

Boa Constrictors

reptiles,
crawls,
no legs

live in rain
forest, need trees to
survive, molts

Bees

insects,
flies,
has legs

1. How are bees and boa constrictors alike in their habitat?

   They both live in the rain forest.

2. As a species, how are bees and boa constrictors different?

   _____

3. Why do both bees and boa constrictors need trees?

   _____

4. Name another difference between bees and boa constrictors.

   _____

B Continue to compare and contrast the boa constrictor and the bee by putting these words in the correct areas:

   lays eggs   pupa   bones   wings   teeth

Superlatives and Comparatives

- Use *-est* to form superlatives and *-er* to form comparatives.

- Comparatives are used with the conjunctions *than* and *but*:

  Al is taller <u>than</u> Marc. Marc is tall, <u>but</u> Sonia is taller.

- Superlatives use the article *the* when only one superlative is in the sentence:

  Masami is <u>the</u> tallest boy in class.

Ⓐ Combine each adjective with the correct suffix to make the superlative or comparative form. The first one has been done for you.

1. What is the comparative form of *slow*? _slower_____

2. What is the superlative form of *mild*? _____

3. What is the comparative form of *nice*? _____

4. What is the superlative form of *bare*? _____

5. What is the superlative form of *calm*? _____

6. What is the comparative form of *cheap*? _____

Ⓑ Using the adjectives *fancy, gentle, grand,* or *meek,* write two sentences using the comparative form and two sentences using the superlative form. Use each adjective only once.

1. _____

2. _____

3. _____

4. _____

Inquiry Checklist: Week 3

Put a check mark next to each item once it is complete.

Share New Information

☐ Each person in my group shared information.

☐ We revised our conjecture if our understandings changed.

☐ We filled in the Idea Tracker for Week 3.

6. Develop Presentation

☐ We chose a format for our presentation.
PRACTICE COMPANION **108, 373**

☐ We talked about how we might use technology in our presentation.

☐ We created the presentation format.

☐ We used the Presentation Organizer to plan our presentation.

☐ We gave a speaking part to each group member.

☐ All group members completed their Week 3 Inquiry Planners.
PRACTICE COMPANION **154**

Notes:

_____

_____

_____

_____

_____

_____

_____

Inquiry Planner: Week 3

Write your group's updated Inquiry Question and conjecture. Then write your Action Plan for next week.

My group's updated Inquiry Question is: _____

_____

My group's updated conjecture is: _____

_____

Action Plan

1. What topics will I collect information for? _____

_____

_____

2. What sources will I use? _____

_____

_____

3. Where will I find these sources? _____

_____

_____

4. When will I collect information? _____

_____

_____

5. How will I record the information? _____

_____

_____

Focus Question: What happens when there are changes to an ecosystem?

What animals did you read about? How did changes to the ecosystem affect this animal? Write your answers in the table below.

Animals	Changes	Effects

How are living things connected? Use examples from your selection to explain your answer.

_____

_____

_____

_____

_____

_____

_____

Focus Question: How do people play a part in ecosystems?

People's actions can affect ecosystems. Think about each of the following actions: *creating an artificial lake, going fishing,* and *planting a tree.* What effect could each action have? Write your answers on the lines below.

An Artificial Lake _____

_____

_____

_____

Going Fishing _____

_____

_____

_____

Planting a Tree _____

_____

_____

My Weekly Planner

Week of _____

Theme Vocabulary	This week's words:
Differentiated Vocabulary	This week's words:
Comprehension Strategy and Skill	This week's comprehension strategy: This week's comprehension skill:
Vocabulary Strategy	This week's vocabulary strategy:
Spelling/Word Study Skill	This week's spelling skill:
Word Study Skill	This week's word study skill:
Fluency	This week's fluency selection:
Writing and Language Arts	This week's writing form:
Grammar	This week's grammar skill:

Word Relationships

Choose two words from the vocabulary list that are related in some way. List the words below and explain the connection between the two. Then write a sentence using both words to explain the connection. You can add word endings if you want.

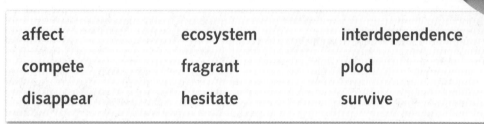

affect	ecosystem	interdependence
compete	fragrant	plod
disappear	hesitate	survive

1. Word Pair: _hesitate, plod_

   Connection: _ways to slow down or stop_

   Sentence: _Because he hesitated to show his report card, he plodded._

2. Word Pair: _____

   Connection: _____

   Sentence: _____

3. Word Pair: _____

   Connection: _____

   Sentence: _____

4. Word Pair: _____

   Connection: _____

   Sentence: _____

5. Word Pair: _____

   Connection: _____

   Sentence: _____

Categories and Classifications

Read the list of words in the box below. Each word fits into one of the categories found in the table. Place the words where they belong.

aroma	shells	interdependence
competing	ocean	smoke
desert	pines	soar
dew	plodding	soil
flowers	rain	steam
hesitating	rain forest	sunlight

Ecosystems	Animal Aids to Survival	Things Plants Need to Grow
Fragrant Things	**Things That Disappear**	**Ways of Moving**

159

Words with VCCCV Pattern

			Frequently misspelled words	Review words
explain	although	pilgrim		
instead	sample	supply		shelter
athlete	surprise	farther	let's	capture
kingdom	address	sandwich		
monster	complete		lets	
orchard	single			

A Fill in the missing letter for each spelling word and cross it off below the box. The first one has been done for you.

ex _p_ lain   ath ___ ete   com ___ lete   sin ___ le

alt ___ ough   sa ___ dwich   or ___ hard   far ___ her

sur ___ rise   supp ___ y   mo ___ ster   sa ___ ple

pil ___ rim   in ___ tead   add ___ ess   king ___ om

n   p̸   h   l   r   p   p   g
s   l   c   n   g   d   m   t

B Divide each spelling word into syllables by drawing a line between the syllables. The first one has been done for you.

1. _ex | plain_____

2. _____

3. _____

4. _____

5. _____

6. _____

7. _____

8. _____

9. _____

10. _____

11. _____

12. _____

13. _____

14. _____

15. _____

16. _____

C **Proofread the paragraph. Insert the correct punctuation in the boxes at the end of each sentence. Circle the misspelled words and write them correctly on the lines below.**

    Once upon a time there was a princess named Elena who lived in a faraway kigndom☐ Althow she had everything she could ever want, what Elena really wanted was to become a great athlet☐ Her father was surprised that this was her dream, but instede of trying to change her mind, he suplied her with all the equipment and training she needed☐ Each morning she would compleet ten laps around the apple orcard☐ With each day, she could run a little farthere down the narow streets☐ Elena explained to her friends that she wanted to be the singl fastest person in the entire kingdom☐ On Pilgram Day, a holiday celebrated throughout the land, she adresed the people of her kingdom, "Lets have a race☐" Elena ran faster than ever before and easily won the race☐ She was the fastest person in the kingdom☐

1. _____

2. _____

3. _____

4. _____

5. _____

6. _____

7. _____

8. _____

9. _____

10. _____

11. _____

12. _____

13. _____

14. _____

Speech

Practice reading this speech to a partner.

Environmental Action

by Holly Young

Are you at all concerned about the state of the environment? Did you know you have an impact, and it's up to you to make it positive or negative? Understanding the impact people have on their environment is the first step toward saving it!

You don't have to wander very far to see the effects we have on the world around us: water pollution, air pollution, and deforestation are affecting the Earth every day. These are big problems. But even the little decisions people make each day have an effect. For example, a simple picnic at the beach can cause complex problems. What if you don't throw away your trash, and instead, leave it behind? Did you know that animals can ingest it or get tangled in it? A small piece of trash can have a big impact.

But all is not lost! There is still much that we can do to save the environment. And that is why I urge you today: Think about what you are doing and the effects that your actions have on the environment. The next time you take a walk and see garbage, pick it up. Throw it away. It's all up to us. We can start today!

Did you read the speech with fluency? Use the form on the next page to evaluate yourself and your partner.

Reading Response Form

A On a scale of 1 to 5, rate yourself and your partner. Do this for the first reading and final readings, at least. On a scale of 1 to 5, 5 is considered outstanding, 3 is good, and 1 is average.

1. Did I …

Read the words correctly?

Read at a good pace?

Read with expression?

Read clearly for my audience?

First Reading	Second Reading	Final Reading

2. Did my partner …

Read the words correctly?

Read at a good pace?

Read with expression?

Read clearly for my audience?

First Reading	Second Reading	Final Reading

B After the first reading, share with your partner how you thought he or she read, and offer suggestions for improvement.

C After the final reading, answer the following questions for yourself.

1. What did I do well?

First Reading _____

Second Reading _____

Final Reading _____

2. What should I do to improve my reading next time?

First Reading _____

Second Reading _____

Final Reading _____

Ask and Answer Questions

Experienced readers **ask and answer questions** before, during, and after their reading.

> When you **ask and answer questions,** you:
>
> - Focus on what you do not understand or what you wonder about in the text
>
> - Look for answers in the text
>
> - Think about your own experiences and any prior knowledge to help you better understand the text

Before Reading

Good readers preview a text before reading it. They look at the title, headings, and pictures. Usually, this preview will lead to questions such as:

- What does the title tell me about the selection?

- Why did the author choose this genre?

During Reading

Questions readers have while they are reading have to do with understanding the text. Questions that a good reader might ask include:

- What does that statement mean?

- Why did the author write the text this way?

- What are some other examples of this subject matter?

After Reading

Questions that a reader may have after reading include things in the text the reader still does not understand, or things brought up in the text that the reader wants to know more about.

You will now read about prairies. Before you begin reading, write questions that you have about prairies in Column 1. As you read, write any questions that you have in Column 2. When you are finished reading, write any remaining questions that you have in Column 3. Once you have completed the chart and the reading, write the answers to your questions in the chart.

Farmland Replaces Buffalo on Prairies

Prairies are found on every continent on Earth except for Antarctica. These flat grasslands have rich soil with large mineral deposits. These minerals make the land ideal for growing crops. A true prairie gets only 20 to 30 inches of rain each year, so the minerals, which make the land so fertile, do not wash away. Year after year, the soil gets richer and richer.

The prairies, however, were not always used as farmland. Before settlers began moving west, the American prairie was just a large expanse of grassland covered with herds of animals such as buffalo. Without people and farms, the buffalo were free to wander the land and live peacefully.

Today, most of the buffalo are gone. Fortunately, some states are working to help the prairies regain some of their native wildlife.

Before Reading	During Reading	After Reading

Master Word Meanings

Many words have meanings beyond their **denotation,** or dictionary definition. For example, the word *mother* has many **connotations** attached to it. Connotation is what you think of when you hear a word or how that word makes you feel.

Phrases can sometimes go beyond their literal meaning. These expressions are known as **idioms.** In order to understand what an idiom means, you have to learn the meanings of various idioms in the same way that you learn the meanings of vocabulary words.

> Read the sentence below.
>
> **You are skating on thin ice if you wait until the last minute to study for your science test.**

You know that skating on thin ice is dangerous. You also know that waiting until the last minute to study for a test is not a good idea. By understanding how words relate to each other, you can figure out that this idiom means "taking a risk."

Look at the idioms and their meanings below. Do the meanings make sense to you?

1. I haven't got a clue.

I am befuddled or puzzled.

2. In the blink of an eye

very fast or immediately.

3. Against the clock

rushed or short on time

4. Once in a blue moon

hardly ever happens or very rare

Read this passage. For each purple underlined word, write the word's denotation and connotation. For each blue underlined idiom, write the idiom's meaning and related words that give you a clue to the idiom's meaning. One of each has been done for you.

My brother is always putting all of his eggs into one basket. When he was younger, he didn't play a lot of different sports. Instead, all he did was swim. He spent all of his free time in our pool. He wanted to be an Olympic swimmer and, knowing that actions speak louder than words, he did nothing but swim. My brother was the apple of my mother's eye and she loved to cheer him on. All of his hard work eventually paid off. He won an Olympic gold medal and we were all very proud of his accomplishment.

1. free time _denotation: time to oneself; leisure time_
   connotation: enjoyment, freedom, relaxation

2. Olympic _____

   _____

3. hard work _____

   _____

4. putting all of his eggs into one basket _meaning: to not have other options_
   related words: all he did was swim

5. actions speak louder than words _____

   _____

6. apple of my mother's eye _____

   _____

Before and After Reading

Before you read the next selection, read the statements below and put a check next to the ones you believe to be true.

Before reading		How a Swamp Was Saved	After reading
		Statement	
		1. Everglades National Park is in a huge swamp.	
		2. Very few plants and animals live in the Everglades.	
		3. People once drained all the water from the Everglades.	
		4. Some people worked hard to protect the Everglades.	

Before reading		Ecosystem Invaders	After reading
		Statement	
		1. Animals sometimes leave their habitats when new animals move in.	
		2. Tiny animals can cling to boats and travel with them to a new lake.	
		3. All pigs live on farms.	
		4. A vine from kudzu can completely cover a house.	

Why Is the World Green?

Before reading	Statement	After reading
	1. Scientists brought wolves to Yellowstone National Park to help the plants and the animals grow.	
	2. Some scientists work outdoors.	
	3. It is important to keep some predators from eating certain plants.	
	4. Some animals eat only plants.	

Island of the Tortoises

Before reading	Statement	After reading
	1. The Galápagos Islands in the Pacific Ocean all have exactly the same plants and animals.	
	2. When people came to the Galápagos Islands long ago, they hunted giant tortoises for food.	
	3. The government of Ecuador has passed laws to protect white-tip reef sharks.	
	4. Plants that farmers brought to the Galápagos Islands destroyed other plants, which native animals used to eat.	

Compare and Contrast

To obtain useful information when you **compare** and **contrast**, you must ask meaningful questions, or questions that relate to the subject you are researching.

> Why were these events held on the different days?

> Which people went to both events?

Read the paragraphs below and then read the sentences that follow. Circle T if the sentence is True and F if the sentence is False.

    Parrots and toucans are both known for their brilliant colors. Perhaps this is why many people mistake toucans for parrots. In truth, there are many differences. Toucans are soft-billed birds, which means they eat mostly fruits. Parrots, which are hard-billed birds, eat seeds and nuts.

    You can also distinguish parrots from toucans by simply looking at their beaks. Toucans have long, often colorful, beaks that extend several inches from their heads. Parrots' beaks, on the other hand, are shorter and curved. Although both toucans and parrots utter a wide variety of barks and croaks, toucans cannot speak or imitate human voices like parrots can.

(T) F **1.** Both toucans and parrots are birds.

T F **2.** Only parrots are colorful.

T F **3.** Toucans eat seeds, but parrots do not.

T F **4.** Both parrots and toucans can imitate human voices.

T F **5.** Toucans have longer beaks than parrots.

T F **6.** Parrots and toucans are known for their brilliant colors.

T F **7.** People often mistake toucans for parrots.

Combining Word Parts

When you add a prefix or a suffix to a root, the prefix or suffix adds a new and more specific focus to the root's meaning.

You can also make an entirely new word by combining two roots. For example, *bio-*, which means "life," takes on the meaning "life-writing" when combined with *-graphy*.

Prefixes:

re-

tri-

Roots: geo

act   bio

eco   cycle

graphy   ology

Suffixes:

-or

-me

-tion

Using the prefixes, roots, and suffixes in the boxes above, combine the appropriate root with the correct prefix, suffix, or other root to complete the statements below. The first statement has been done for you.

1. A(n) *actor* _____ performs on a stage.

2. _____ is the study of rocks.

3. A(n) _____ has three wheels.

4. When you _____ plastic and paper, people will be able to use them again.

5. _____ is the study of the environments.

6. A(n) _____ is about a person's life.

7. The _____ on the field was so fast.

8. We studied mountains in _____.

9. You must _____ quickly in emergencies.

10. _____ is the study of living things.

Inquiry Checklist: Week 4

Put a check mark next to each item once it is complete.

Share New Information

☐ Each person in my group shared information.

☐ We revised our conjecture if our understandings changed.

7. Deliver Presentation

☐ We rehearsed our presentation.

☐ We presented for another group.

☐ We used the Presentation Rubric to evaluate our own presentation.

☐ We used the Presentation Rubric to evaluate the other group's presentation.

☐ We received feedback. We used the Presentation Organizer to revise our presentation.

Identify New Questions

☐ All group members listed new questions on their Week 4 Inquiry Planners.

PRACTICE COMPANION 173

☐ We posted new questions on the Question Board.

Notes:

_____

_____

_____

_____

_____

_____

_____

Inquiry Planner: Week 4

Write your plans for investigating new questions.

1. What other questions do I want to investigate? _____
_____
_____
_____

2. What sources can I use? _____
_____
_____
_____

3. Where will I find these sources? _____
_____
_____
_____

4. When will I collect information? _____
_____
_____
_____

Self-Assessment Rubric

Read each goal in the chart. Make a check mark to give yourself a score of 3, 2, or 1. Then complete the sentences below.

Category	Goals	Very Good 3	OK 2	Needs Work 1
Group Role	I understood and fulfilled my role.			
Participation	I helped my group complete each step of the Inquiry Process.			
Research	I did research on my own and shared it with my group.			
Listening	I gave others a chance to speak and listened well.			
Collaboration	I shared my ideas and respected others' ideas.			
Responsibility	I stayed on task during group work.			
Presentation	I was prepared for our presentation. I spoke clearly and effectively.			
Enjoyment	I enjoyed working with others in my group.			

1. One thing I did well was: _____

_____

2. One thing I would like to improve is: _____

_____

Think about the roles people played in the ecosystem you read about. In what ways did people help or harm the ecosystem? Fill in the chart with your answers.

Help	Harm

How are living things connected? Use examples from your selection to explain your answer.

_____

_____

_____

_____

_____

_____

_____

_____

Study the Model
Compare and Contrast Essay
Read the Writing Model along with your teacher. Look for the transition words and vivid vocabulary.

Life in the Desert and Rain Forest
by Alex Linfield

The tropical rain forest offers a humid, warm climate and lush vegetation. On the other hand, animals and plants that live in the desert survive in its extremely hot and dry conditions. At first glance these two places couldn't be more different, but there are a number of similarities too.

The rain forest and desert climates are very different. Deserts are found in areas that receive very little rain. Rain forests receive more rain than deserts. In contrast to the lush, green landscape of the tropical rain forest, the desert is mostly covered in sand and dry soil. While the trees of the tropical rain forest stretch toward the sky, the plants and trees of the desert are smaller and are able to conserve water.

Both the tropical rain forest and the desert are home to many animals. The rain of the rain forest makes it a perfect habitat for a variety of insects, reptiles, amphibians, and mammals. The desert is home to animals such as coyotes, jack rabbits, and mice, which are able to tolerate heat.

Animals and plants of both habitats have adapted to the extreme conditions of their surroundings. Some animals of the rain forest climb high up in the trees for food and protection, while others survive on the forest floor. Similarly, animals in the desert stay hidden during the day to avoid the heat and come out nightly to gather food and water.

Though tropical rain forests and deserts have their differences, one thing is certain: when night falls on the rain forest as well as the desert, the chirps and howls of animals can be heard for miles! Both habitats are home to many interesting plants and animals, and taking care of these majestic places means people can learn about them for many years to come.

Evaluation Rubric

Compare and Contrast Essay

Writing Traits	Goals	Yes	Needs Work!	Now it's OK.
Organization	I have an introduction and a conclusion. Each body paragraph compares or contrasts the topic.			
Ideas	Details show how the subjects are the same and different. My ideas are clearly expressed in each paragraph.			
Voice	My essay sounds like I wrote it.			
Word Choice	I used vivid words.			
Sentence Fluency	I used transition words that signal comparison and contrast. My sentences and paragraphs flow smoothly.			
Conventions	I used capital letters at the beginning of each sentence and for all proper nouns. I used correct punctuation. All the words are spelled correctly.			

Compare and Contrast Essay

Peer Review

Read your partner's paper. Then finish each sentence.

1. I see that this compare and contrast essay is organized by _____

   _____

   _____

   _____

2. Some details that the author uses to compare and contrast are _____

   _____

   _____

   _____

3. Some transition words that the author might include are _____

   _____

   _____

   _____

Name of Reader _____

Adverbs That Tell *How*

When adverbs modify verbs, they can tell how something happens. Adverbs that tell *how* are sometimes called "adverbs of manner."

Question	Answer
How did the chorus sing?	The chorus sang beautifully.
How does my sister laugh?	My sister laughs loudly.
How do you play?	I play well.
How does he run?	He runs fast.

A **Look at the sentences. Underline the adverb of manner and double underline the verb it modifies. The first one has been done for you.**

1. Janice skipped happily along the sidewalk.
2. Each morning, the sparrow merrily chirps outside my window.
3. Lucy carefully studied the instructions for the project.
4. Tyrone is reading quietly in the library.
5. Quickly the cougar sprints across the plain.

B **Write a sentence using the adverbs of manner from the list below. The first one has been done for you.**

cheerfully	closely	healthy	correctly	easily

1. *My little brother cheerfully ate his cereal.*
2. _____
3. _____
4. _____
5. _____

Adverbs That Tell *When* and *Where*

When adverbs modify verbs, they can tell when or where. Adverbs can be found in different parts of the sentence, not just near verbs.

> **Tom arrived late for school.**
>
> The adverb *late* tells when. It modifies the verb *arrived*.

> **The restaurant is nearby.**
>
> The adverb *nearby* tells where. It modifies the verb *is*.

A Complete each sentence by writing an adverb that tells when or where. The first one has been done for you.

1. The cat ran. (where) *The cat ran inside.*

2. The class will eat lunch. (when) _____

3. Henry brushes his teeth. (when) _____

4. Katherine played. (where) _____

B Write new sentences using the adverbs you chose in Part A. The first one has been done for you.

1. *I stay inside during thunderstorms.*

2. _____

3. _____

4. _____

C Underline the adverb. Then write whether the adverb is telling when or where. The first one has been done for you.

1. The rain has gone <u>away</u>. *where*

2. I recently went to the zoo. _____

3. Sonia usually says hello. _____

4. Deng brushed the dog aside. _____

5. Our parrot never talks. _____

Use -er and -est to Compare

Adjectives sometimes change their form to show different degrees. Use -er
to show comparative degree and -est to show superlative degree.

Adjective	Comparative	Superlative
long	longer	longest
wise	wiser	wisest
angry	angrier	angriest
gentle	gentler	gentlest

- If the adjective ends in -y, change the -y to i before adding -er
  or -est.

- If the adjective ends in -le, add -r for the comparative form and
  -st for the superlative form.

**Choose the word that best completes each sentence. Write it on the
line. The first one has been done for you.**

1. My older brother is (stronger, strongest) than I am. _stronger_

2. The new refrigerator works (better, best) than the old one. _____

3. This is the (prettier, prettiest) ring I have ever seen. _____

4. The broccoli is the (healthier, healthiest) food on the plate. _____

5. A cheetah can run (faster, fastest) than a house cat. _____

6. Who is the (taller, tallest) student on the team? _____

7. Ryan's sandwich is (thickest, thicker) than Monica's. _____

8. The sun shines (hotter, hottest) in the afternoon. _____

9. This is the (deeper, deepest) part of the lake. _____

10. Ngo is the (happy, happier, happiest) student in our school. _____

11. Milo is (busy, busier, busiest) than Thule. _____

12. I think that cats are (gentler, gentlest) than dogs. _____

Use *More/Most* to Compare

Use *more* or *most* instead of *-er* or *-est* when an adjective has two or more syllables and does not end in *-y, -er, -le,* or *-ow.* You form the comparative using the word *more* and the superlative using the word *most.*

Andrew Jackson

$700

George Washington

$2,220

Abraham Lincoln

$1,250

Abraham Lincoln's autograph is more expensive than Andrew Jackson's. George Washington's autograph is the most expensive.

Read each adjective. Write a sentence using the adjective and either the comparative *more* or the superlative *most.* The first one has been done for you.

1. interesting *This is the most interesting book I have ever read.*

2. delicious _____

3. furious _____

4. beautiful _____

5. patient _____

6. polite _____

7. satisfying _____

8. delightful _____

Using Test-Taking Strategies

Sometimes, instead of choosing an answer to a test question, you must write your own answer. Here is a sample question based on *The Great Kapok Tree.*

Sample Question:

Describe the great Kapok tree in the selection. Use information from the selection to support your answer.

Look carefully at what the prompt asks you to do:

- You must describe the great Kapok tree.

- You must choose information from the text that best supports, or makes clear, your description.

There are different ways to address this prompt. Here are some possible answers:

- The tree is very large. The text says "the great Kapok tree shoots up through the forest and emerges above the canopy."

- The tree is tall and has a thick trunk. You can tell that from the picture on page 349.

- The tree is huge and has very hard wood. You can tell that because the man has a difficult time chopping it down.

When you write your own answer, check your answer. Be sure that you do everything the question asks you to do.

Applying Test-Taking Strategies

Now carefully read the prompt below. Think about what you need
to do to address the prompt completely.

**The animals in *The Great Kapok Tree* give reasons why the man should
not cut down the tree. Choose three of their reasons, and tell how they
are like the ideas you read about in *Balance in the Wild*.**

**Use information from the selections to complete the chart below and
plan your response. Then on a separate sheet of paper write a paragraph
that uses this information to answer the prompt.**

Reason animal gives not to chop down the tree ...	... is like this idea from *Balance in the Wild*
The bee pollinates the trees and flowers throughout the rain forest, and shows how all living things depend on each other.	Every part of an ecosystem does a certain job and all living things are connected to each other through the jobs that they do.

My Weekly Planner

Week of _____

Theme Vocabulary	This week's words:
Differentiated Vocabulary	This week's words:
Comprehension Strategy and Skill	This week's comprehension strategy: This week's comprehension skill:
Vocabulary Strategy	This week's vocabulary strategy:
Spelling/Word Study Skill	This week's spelling skill:
Word Study Skill	This week's word study skill:
Fluency	This week's fluency selection:
Writing and Language Arts	This week's writing form:
Grammar	This week's grammar skills:

Complete the Paragraph

Use words from the word bank to complete the paragraph below.
You will use three words twice.

extremes	irrigation	spectacular
arid	tundra	

Earth has many _____ environments.
The heat, cold, or lack of rainfall makes these environments
some of the hardest places to live. In the North American

_____, farming is not possible because it is

bitterly cold for much of the year and the soil is thin. Native peoples

of the _____ live off the sea and land

animals, including fish and _____ herds of

caribou. In desert regions, on the other hand, life can be hard

because of the _____ climate. People

can farm in some desert regions, but usually only with the help of

_____ to bring water to the fields.

Antarctica is the coldest place on Earth. Freezing temperatures, ice,

and snow are _____ of the region. The only

people who live in Antarctica are scientists. Most only stay there

part-time, but they get to enjoy Antarctica's

_____

scenery, which includes towering mountains, vast ice sheets,

and active volcanoes.

Word Skeletons

Complete the word skeletons below.

1.

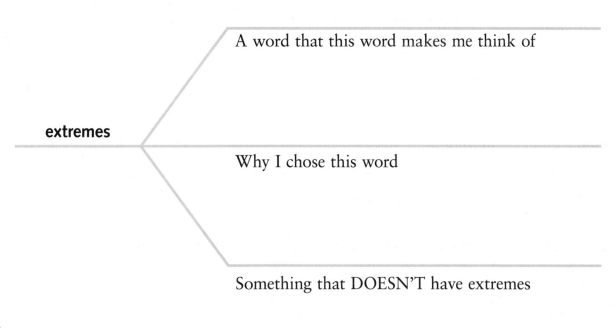

extremes

A word that this word makes me think of

Why I chose this word

Something that DOESN'T have extremes

2.

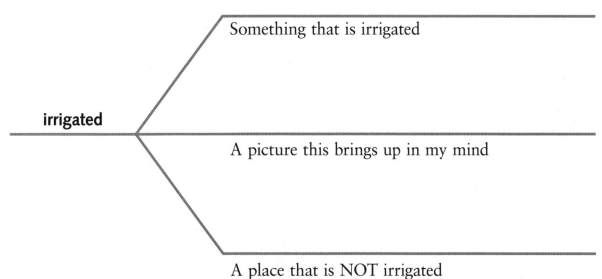

irrigated

Something that is irrigated

A picture this brings up in my mind

A place that is NOT irrigated

Words with Double Vowels

			Frequently misspelled words	Review words
idea	India	cereal		
lion	piano	video		
usual	fuel	meteor		explain
radio	diary	February	they're	sandwich
liar	violin		right	
poem	period			

A Unscramble the words below. Write the correct spelling on the line.

1. eFbraruy _____

2. eluf _____

3. riady _____

4. deia _____

5. ghirt _____

6. uuals _____

7. aoidr _____

8. rlia _____

9. Iinda _____

10. apnio _____

11. mope _____

12. linvio _____

13. repiod _____

14. eaelrc _____

15. odive _____

16. niol _____

17. re'heyt _____

B Proofread the paragraph. In the boxes at the end of each sentence, place the correct punctuation. Circle the misspelled words and write the correct spelling on the lines below.

My friends and I had an idia for a survey that we wanted to give our class☐ We put the survey together in Febuery after watching a vidao in class☐ Our survey asked several questions:

What is your favorite breakfast cerael☐ What kind of radoi station do you listen to☐ Do you write in a diery☐ Have you ever written a pome☐ Would you rather learn to play the paino or the voilin☐

There were no rihgt or wrong answers but we were curious to see what our classmates said☐ We think the're going to be surprised by the results☐

1. _____

2. _____

3. _____

4. _____

5. _____

6. _____

7. _____

8. _____

9. _____

10. _____

11. _____

Advertisement

Practice reading this advertisement to a partner.

The Great Potato State

by Will Howard

The state of Idaho brings to mind a swirl of images: snow-covered mountains, green forests, and sparkling lakes. Many people think of potatoes when they think of Idaho. All of these images represent important features of this mountain state.

Idaho's natural resources are at the heart of its economy. The southern part of the state, where it breaks free from the Rocky Mountains, contains most of the state's farmland. In the valleys of the Snake River, Idaho grows one-third of the country's whole potato crop. That's a lot of spuds!

Although Idaho has a large farming community, it is also home to a robust manufacturing trade and tourism industry. Factories turn out food products, wood products, and technology—to name just a few. Tourism is also growing in Idaho. People love to visit and enjoy all that the state's geography offers.

No matter when you come to visit Idaho, you will be delighted. The mountains and forests, potatoes and tourist locales are waiting for you!

Did you read the advertisement with fluency? Use the form on the next page to evaluate yourself and your partner.

Reading Response Form

A On a scale of 1 to 5, rate yourself and your partner. Do this for the first reading and final readings, at least. On a scale of 1 to 5, 5 is considered outstanding, 3 is good, and 1 is average.

1. Did I ...

	First Reading	Second Reading	Final Reading
Read the words correctly?			
Read at a good pace?			
Read with expression?			
Read clearly for my audience?			

2. Did my partner ...

	First Reading	Second Reading	Final Reading
Read the words correctly?			
Read at a good pace?			
Read with expression?			
Read clearly for the audience?			

B After the first reading, share with your partner how you thought he or she read, and offer suggestions for improvement.

C After the final reading, answer the following questions for yourself.

1. What did I do well?

First Reading _____

Second Reading _____

Final Reading _____

2. What should I do to improve my reading next time?

First Reading _____

Second Reading _____

Final Reading _____

Visualize

What does it mean to visualize while reading?

When you **visualize**, you use the words on the page to create pictures in your mind. You picture the people, places, and things the author describes.

Why should you visualize while reading?

Visualizing helps you see, feel, and hear what the author describes. When you visualize, you can imagine being a part of the story.

Step 1   Look for word clues in a passage that signal it might be a good time to visualize:

- Descriptive words
- Actions
- Comparisons

Step 2   Think about your own experiences. Use the passage and your own ideas to create a picture in your mind.

Step 3   As you read on, use new information from the passage to add to or change your mental picture.

Read the passage and then answer the questions.

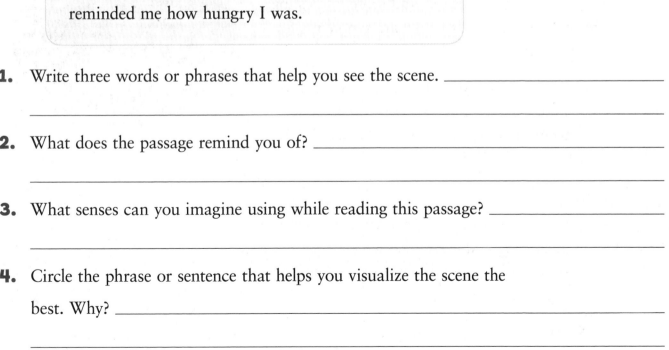

The crows made a racket in the trees. That's what woke me up. It was hardly even light out. "I stayed up way too late," I grunted to myself. I unzipped my sleeping bag, and even the chilly air didn't help shake the cobwebs out of my head. Shivering, I crawled out and got dressed as quickly as I could. I shuffled out of my tent, yawning.

The others were already up. The fire crackled, and I held my hands out to warm them. I put a pan of water over the flames, and as soon as it was warm, I took it to the stream and washed up. The warm and cold water splashing on my face made me feel human again. I went back to the campsite. Now the early morning sun winked through pines. The smell of bacon, smoke, toast reminded me how hungry I was.

1. Write three words or phrases that help you see the scene. _____

_____

2. What does the passage remind you of? _____

_____

3. What senses can you imagine using while reading this passage? _____

_____

4. Circle the phrase or sentence that helps you visualize the scene the

best. Why? _____

_____

Synonyms

A **synonym** is a word that has the same or almost the same meaning as another word. Synonyms are useful for both reading and writing. You can use synonyms to help you understand unfamiliar words. You can also use synonyms to make your writing more interesting. You can find synonyms for a word in a dictionary or a thesaurus.

> You can use synonyms to help you better understand a word that is new to you. Below is a definition of the word *massive*. Look for familiar words in the definition, like the words highlighted below. Think of synonyms for the words you know.
>
> - **massive,** *adjective*: very big; large and solid
>
>   **synonyms**: huge, gigantic

> You can use synonyms to figure out unfamiliar words. Authors often use synonyms in their writing to make their ideas clearer and more interesting. The highlighted words below are synonyms for the word *devastated*.
>
> - The hurricane devastated the county. Many homes were completely destroyed. Even large office buildings were badly damaged. Power lines were ruined.

> You can use synonyms to make your own writing more interesting and clear. The sentences below are an example of how you might use synonyms to express your ideas better.
>
> - The game was a triumph for the hard-luck baseball team. The win was the first victory for the team in three straight seasons!

A Read each word and its definition. Underline familiar words in the definition. Then write two synonyms for each word on the line. You may use a dictionary or thesaurus to help you.

1. **devour,** *v.*: eat hungrily or quickly

   _____

2. **comic,** *adj.*: causing laughter

   _____

B Read the following sentences. In each item, underline a synonym for the highlighted word. Then write your own definition for the word.

1. At dusk we all gathered on the shore to watch the boats leave before sunset.

   My definition: _____

2. Manny didn't mean to distress his mother by not calling to say he would be late. When he got home, he said he was sorry that he worried her so.

   My definition: _____

C Choose one of the words from the box. Write a synonym for your word. You may use a dictionary or thesaurus to help you. Then write a sentence that uses the word you chose and its synonym.

dilemma	abundant	grateful
elegant	fortunate	odd

My Word: _____

Synonym: _____

My Sentence: _____

_____

_____

Generalize

When you **generalize**, you make a broad statement about examples that have something in common. Look at the chart below to help you make generalizations as you read.

How to Generalize

Look for the overall message of the selection.	Think about what you already know about the topic.	Write a generalization.

Read the paragraph below.

> Yellowstone National Park was the first national park in the United States. It is quite large, covering land in the Western States of Wyoming, Montana, and Idaho. Inside the park, visitors can see hot springs, famous geysers, and spectacular wildlife. If you are planning to visit Yellowstone, make sure to look for the stunning elk, grizzly bears, and bison that roam the park. You just might see them!

Now, think about what you already know about the topic and what you learned from the paragraph to write a generalization.

_____

_____

Prefixes

Prefixes are word parts added to the beginning of a word. You can use the meaning of a prefix to help you figure out the meaning of a word. The prefixes below all mean "not" or "opposite."

un-   dis-   mis-   de-   counter-

A Add one of the prefixes listed above to the words below to make a new word.

1. _____ clockwise

2. _____ happy

3. _____ take

4. _____ frost

5. _____ appear

B Add one of the prefixes to the words below to complete the sentences.

1. My mother had to _____ wrap the gift.

2. My teacher had to _____ connect the wire.

3. The train will _____ part from Track 12.

4. We will move in a _____ clockwise direction.

5. Sabrina often _____ spells the word *their*.

Inquiry Checklist: Week 1

Put a check mark next to each item once it is complete.

Discussion Roles

☐ I took a role in my group.

PRACTICE COMPANION 370

My role is _____.

1. Generate Ideas and Questions

☐ We thought of at least three possible questions.

☐ We chose an Inquiry Question to investigate.

2. Make a Conjecture

☐ We shared what we know about our Inquiry Question.

☐ We made a conjecture about our Inquiry Question.

☐ We filled in the Idea Tracker for Week 1.

☐ We posted our Inquiry Question and conjecture on the Question Board.

3. Make Plans to Collect Information

☐ We made a list of topics to research and split them up among the group.

☐ We used the Information Finder and made a list of possible sources to use.

PRACTICE COMPANION 371

☐ All group members completed their Week 1 Inquiry Planners.

PRACTICE COMPANION 199

Notes:

_____

_____

_____

_____

Inquiry Planner: Week 1

Write your group's Inquiry Question and conjecture. Then write your Action Plan for next week.

My group's Inquiry Question is: _____

_____

My group's conjecture is: _____

_____

Action Plan

1. What topics will I collect information for? _____

_____

_____

2. What sources will I use? _____

_____

_____

3. Where will I find these sources? _____

_____

_____

4. When will I collect information? _____

_____

_____

5. How will I record the information? _____

_____

_____

Time Line

Read about time lines and study the example.

What is a time line?

- A time line is a graphic that shows a series of events that includes the date and a description of each event.

- It has a start and end date at each end.

- Events may be listed from left to right or from top to bottom.

- It may include photos or illustrations to illustrate events.

Important Events in Alaska's History

| Asians migrate from Asia to Alaska. | Russians claim the land and become fur traders. | William Seward purchases Alaska from Russia. | Gold is discovered and many people rush to Alaska. | Alaska becomes the 49th State. | Transatlantic Pipeline is completed. |

B.C. — **1977**

| 30,000– 10,000 B.C. | 1741 | 1867 | 1896 | 1959 | 1977 |

You Can Use Technology

Find out how technology can help you create and share your presentation.

- Log on to **www.wgLEAD21.com.**

- From My Home Page, click on Inquiry Project.

Focus Question: How are geography and economy connected in the Mountain States?

List some of the ways the geographical feature you read about helps the economy of the Mountain States. Judging by what you read about in your selection, how are geography and economy connected in the Mountain States? Fill in the chart below with your answers.

Geographical Feature	How it Connects to the Economy

What makes the West exceptional? Use examples from your selection or your prior knowledge to write your answer on the lines below.

_____

_____

_____

_____

_____

_____

_____

Focus Question: How are geography and economy connected in the Pacific States?

Think about the following: *the Pacific Ocean, miles of beaches,* and *a warm climate.* **How do these things help the economy of the Pacific States? Write your answers on the lines below.**

The Pacific Ocean

_____

_____

_____

Miles of Beaches

_____

_____

_____

A Warm Climate

_____

_____

_____

My Weekly Planner

Week of _____

Theme Vocabulary	This week's words:
Differentiated Vocabulary	This week's words:
Comprehension Strategy and Skill	This week's comprehension strategy: This week's comprehension skill:
Vocabulary Strategy	This week's vocabulary strategy:
Spelling/Word Study Skill	This week's spelling skill:
Word Study Skill	This week's word study skill:
Fluency	This week's fluency selection:
Writing and Language Arts	This week's writing form:
Grammar	This week's grammar skills:

Complete Sentences

A **Draw a line to match the sentence with the word that best completes it.**

1. Spanish _____ tried to get the Aztecs to become Christians.

film

2. Kevin couldn't understand his teenage sister's _____. It seemed she could be laughing one minute and crying the next.

rugged

substantial

3. Anybody can _____ Grandpa sleeping. It takes a true artist to make it something people would want to watch.

dominant

4. The kangaroo rat never has to drink water, which makes it well suited to _____ environments.

irrigated

5. The climb to the top of the bell tower was _____, but the view was amazing.

missionaries

6. The ancient Egyptians _____ their fields with floodwater from the Nile River.

extremes

7. Mr. Wolf, the richest man in town, made his _____ fortune making canned fruit.

arid

8. The Lakeside Rangers had the tallest boys. No wonder they were _____ in basketball.

B **Complete the sentences to show you understand the meaning of the highlighted word.**

1. After his hike through the rugged foothills, Cyrus _____

_____

2. Rebecca prepared for her missionary work by _____

_____

3. One thing I've learned in Hollywood is that if you want to film a movie, the first thing you need is a _____

_____

Vocabulary Recording Sheet

Fill in the Vocabulary Recording Sheet.

Word	What It Means	My Sentence with the Word	Two Related Words
missionaries			
film			
rugged			
substantial			
dominant			

Words with Final *Schwa* + *l* Sound

			Frequently misspelled words	Review words
towel	eagle	barrel		
pedal	special	squirrel	around	violin
riddle	trouble	model		cereal
metal	marvel	tangle	having	
simple	gravel			
ankle	gentle			

A Find the sixteen spelling words hidden in the puzzle.

S	T	A	N	G	L	E	F	R	D	G	A	R	M
I	S	B	A	R	R	E	L	O	W	R	H	I	O
M	T	Q	S	P	E	C	I	A	L	A	O	D	D
P	E	R	U	E	D	R	C	D	Y	V	N	D	E
L	A	U	O	I	E	V	E	L	E	E	E	L	L
E	T	R	G	U	R	E	A	N	K	L	E	E	M
P	A	O	D	T	B	R	H	M	V	I	Z	G	A
B	D	D	W	E	S	L	E	R	N	R	G	S	R
R	I	N	J	E	R	Y	E	L	A	R	T	I	V
J	G	E	N	T	L	E	E	A	G	L	E	L	E
Q	M	E	T	A	L	Y	E	P	E	D	A	L	L

B Proofread the passage. Circle the misspelled words and write them on the lines below.

Maurice was heving some troubble with his ankl. He had twisted it somehow on the pedel of his bike and he marvaled at how it still bothered him after two days. As he walked up his graval driveway, he tried to think of a way to make it feel better.

Suddenly a noise came from a mettal barel that sat next to his garage. Maurice peered in and saw that a squirel had gotten tagnled in a towell at the bottom of the barrel. It couldn't get out. Being very gentl, Maurice tilted the barrel on its side and the squirrel was able to free itself. As it ran away, Maurice noticed it seemed to hobble a little on its left foot. This made Maurice smile. He knew he would be able to recognize this speciel squirrel because it had a bad ankle as well!

1. _____
2. _____
3. _____
4. _____
5. _____
6. _____
7. _____
8. _____
9. _____
10. _____
11. _____
12. _____
13. _____

Procedural Text

Practice reading these directions to a partner.

Hiking in Redwood

by International Parks

Welcome to Redwood National Park! Today you will hike the park's southern trail. Refer to your maps as you hike along the paths. Your starting point is the Prairie Creek Visitor Center, and your destination is Lyons Ranch.

1. From the front of the Visitor Center, look for the sign to your left that says "Elk Prairie." Start walking along the dirt road as it climbs between the stately redwood trees, for about one-half mile. The steep path will curve around to your right when you reach May Creek.

2. The path now loops southward along the creek for one mile. Watch for the sign that says "Elk Meadow." The meadow is perfect for enjoying your lunch at rustic picnic tables beneath giant trees.

3. Now it is decision time! Choose the scenic Coastal Trail if you want to hike toward the Gold Bluffs. From the top of the bluffs, you will have an incredible view of the rolling Pacific Ocean. This trail curls north and ends at the Visitor Center.

4. If you select Bald Hills Road, you will arrive at the Redwood Creek Overlook, one of the highest points in the park. The road winds along a hilltop prairie, ending at historic Lyons Ranch.

Did you read the directions with fluency? Use the form on the next page to evaluate yourself and your partner.

Reading Response Form

A On a scale of 1 to 5, rate yourself and your partner. Do this for the first reading and final readings, at least. On a scale of 1 to 5, 5 is considered outstanding, 3 is good, and 1 is average.

1. Did I …

	First Reading	Second Reading	Final Reading
Read the words correctly?			
Read at a good pace?			
Read with expression?			
Read clearly for my audience?			

2. Did my partner …

	First Reading	Second Reading	Final Reading
Read the words correctly?			
Read at a good pace?			
Read with expression?			
Read clearly for the audience?			

B After the first reading, share with your partner how you thought he or she read, and offer suggestions for improvement.

C After the final reading, answer the following questions for yourself.

1. What did I do well?

First Reading _____

Second Reading _____

Final Reading _____

2. What should I do to improve my reading next time?

First Reading _____

Second Reading _____

Final Reading _____

Monitor Comprehension

At some point, all readers have trouble understanding something they read. **Monitoring comprehension** helps readers notice when they don't understand something.

Fix-up strategies are a key part of monitoring comprehension. The list below gives you six useful fix-up strategies.

- **Reread** the section.

- **Keep reading** to see if the author explains further.

- **Slow down** so you don't miss important information.

- **Speed up.** Reading one word at a time makes it difficult to put ideas together.

- **Use the pictures** to see if they show what the text says.

- **Seek help.** Use a dictionary. Ask someone to help you.

After using one or more fix-up strategies, ask yourself:
Now do I understand? If not, try another fix-up strategy.

Stuck?
Use a fix-up strategy:
- Reread.
- Read on.
- Adjust reading rate.
- Use images.
- Seek help.

I get it!
Keep reading.

I am still confused.
Try another fix-up strategy.

Read the passage below. Circle a sentence that you think is difficult to understand. Write down a fix-up strategy to help you understand the sentence. If the strategy works, write a summary of the sentence in the box on the right. If it doesn't work, try another strategy.

Have you ever seen a person on the sidewalk playing music? Or break dancing? Or putting on a puppet show? Or even standing still, pretending to be a statue? Many performers like to perform on the street. This kind of performing is called busking. Most buskers perform for money. People give them tips if they're enjoying the show.

Today buskers appear at festivals and in cities across the country. Attend the Northwest Folklife Festival in Seattle to hear a whole block of musicians jamming. Visit San Francisco to see jugglers, magicians, and acrobats. No matter where you travel, you are likely to see a busker.

Fix-up strategy	My summary
Fix-up strategy	My summary
Fix-up strategy	My summary

Context Clues

Context clues are words in a text that can be used to help you understand the meaning of an unfamiliar word.

Some context clues give the **meaning** of the word. These context clues often use the word *is* or *are* to hint that the meaning is coming. The highlighted words in the sentence below tell the meaning of the word *entomologist*.

- An **entomologist** is a person who studies insects.

Sometimes a context clue can be a **word or phrase** located next to the unfamiliar word. The highlighted phrase next to the word *species* explains its meaning.

- Not all insects belong to the same **species**, a group of plants or animals with similar traits.

Some context clues are **synonyms** or **antonyms.** A synonym has the same or almost the same meaning as another word. An antonym has the opposite meaning of another word. The synonyms and antonyms for the word *dispersal* are highlighted in the sentences below.

- Many plants rely on seed **dispersal** for survival. This scattering of seeds by birds, animals, and even people ensures that new plants grow in a variety of places. When seeds gather in one place, the young plants may be too crowded to grow.

Read the following passage.

One thousand feet below Mexico's Chihuahua Desert, a team of scientists is studying the stunning mineral formations in the Cave of Crystals. But every trip to the cave could result in tragedy. Why? The scalding conditions in the cave make it deadly to humans. The extreme heat is caused by melted rock called magma that lies under the cave.

Visitors must suit up before their journey to the caverns. First, they don a vest lined with ice packs. Next, they put on another vest to keep out the heat. Their last layer is a bright-orange jumpsuit. They strap on a helmet with a lamp and fit a breathing mask over their face. Finally, they put on gloves and boots.

Use context clues from the passage to write a definition for each word listed. Then write your own sentence using the word.

1. crystals _____

_____

2. tragedy _____

_____

3. scalding _____

_____

4. magma _____

_____

5. don _____

_____

Cause and Effect

Remember, a **cause** is something that makes something else happen. An **effect** is what happens as a result of the cause.

Read the effect in the box on the right and write your own cause for each effect.

Cause	Effect
	Ava broke her arm.

Cause	Effect
	We went in the house.

Cause	Effect
	The girls won their soccer game.

Contractions

Remember, a **contraction** is a short way to write two words together. You use an apostrophe (') to replace some of the letters.

would have = would've

have not = haven't

I had = I'd

A Write a contraction for the two words. The first one has been done for you.

1. I would = ___I'd___

2. had not = _____

3. would not = _____

4. I have = _____

5. she had = _____

B Write the two words for the contraction. The first one has been done for you.

1. hasn't = ___has not___

2. could've = _____

3. we'd = _____

4. didn't = _____

5. shouldn't = _____

Inquiry Checklist: Week 2

Put a check mark next to each item once it is complete.

Collect Information

☐ I used the Evaluating Sources Checklist to check my sources.

PRACTICE COMPANION 372

☐ I recorded information from at least one good source using an Investigation Sheet.

4. Organize and Synthesize Information

☐ Each person in my group shared information.

☐ We organized the information using the Chain Organizer or another type of organizer.

☐ We synthesized the information and found at least one new idea.

5. Confirm or Revise Your Conjecture

☐ We used our new understandings to decide if we should revise our conjecture or our Inquiry Question.

☐ We filled in the Idea Tracker for Week 2.

☐ We posted our revised Inquiry Question and conjecture on the Question Board.

☐ All group members completed their Week 2 Inquiry Planners.

PRACTICE COMPANION 217

Notes:

_____

_____

_____

_____

_____

Inquiry Planner: Week 2

Write your group's updated Inquiry Question and conjecture. Then write your Action Plan for next week.

My group's updated Inquiry Question is: _____

_____

My group's updated conjecture is: _____

_____

Action Plan

1. What topics will I collect information for? _____

_____

_____

2. What sources will I use? _____

_____

_____

3. Where will I find these sources? _____

_____

_____

4. When will I collect information? _____

_____

_____

5. How will I record the information? _____

_____

_____

Think Back
Selection 2

Make a list of the industries you read about in your selection. How do these industries help you understand how geography and economy are connected in the Pacific States?

Industries	Geography Connected to Economy

What makes the West exceptional? Use examples from your selection or your prior knowledge of the West to answer the question on the lines below.

_____

_____

_____

_____

_____

_____

_____

_____

Think about the following: *farming*, *ranching*, and *mining*. What do these industries tell us about life in the Mountain States?

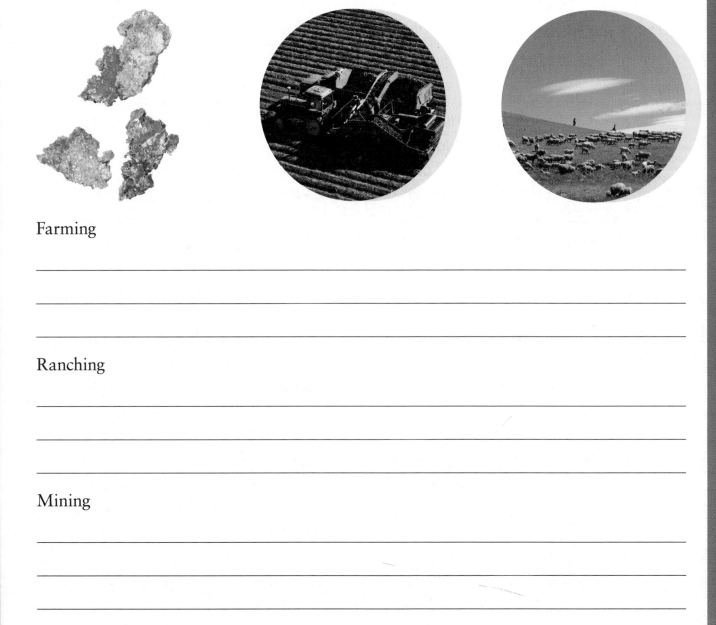

Farming

_____

_____

_____

Ranching

_____

_____

_____

Mining

_____

_____

_____

Study the Model

Science Fiction

Read the Writing Model along with your teacher. Look for the conflict and the way the central character resolves it.

The Thief of the Northwest

by Tony Russo

"Someone is stealing our carrots," I said to my father. It was our first summer in the Northwest Greenhouse, and the carrot patch was my responsibility. Every day a few carrots went missing from the edge of our garden plot.

Dad was alarmed. "We need those carrots, Miko," he said. "If we don't have a good crop, people in the Northwest won't stay healthy. Protecting those carrots is more important than anything else!"

"Let's sleep outside tonight," I suggested. "We can wait and catch the thief red-handed." I had an idea who the thief was: our neighbor on the planet Mariela. After gardening school, I often saw her staring longingly at our enticing crop of carrots. Her task in the spacious greenhouse was growing cabbage, but she had told me once that carrots were the tastiest of all vegetables.

That night, Dad and I spread out our flannel sleeping bags in the garden behind our little cabin. The nights in the Northwest Greenhouse were spectacular and balmy, with a clear view of the stars sprinkled across the sky—much clearer than the polluted haze that had dogged our time in California. I missed living on Earth, but I did not miss the skies clouded with smog.

Soon after falling asleep, I heard a rustling sound. I slipped out of my sleeping bag and crept toward the garden. Suddenly, I turned on my flashlight and saw … the most adorable red space rabbit! It disappeared with a flash. I smiled. I was relieved that I hadn't wrongly accused our neighbor of thievery. At the end of the summer, I put a bushel of carrots outside her door.

Evaluation Rubric

Science Fiction

Writing Traits	Goals	Yes	Needs Work!	Now it's OK.
Organization	My story has a clear beginning, middle, and end.			
	My story has a problem and a solution.			
Ideas	My story involves science, technology, the future, or outer space.			
	I develop interesting characters.			
Voice	My beginning will capture readers.			
	I craft a suspenseful story and include an exciting climax.			
Word Choice	I use vivid descriptive words to describe the setting.			
Sentence Fluency	My sentences flow smoothly from one to the next.			
	I use a variety of sentence lengths.			
Conventions	I use correct punctuation.			
	I use prepositions correctly.			
	All the words are spelled correctly.			
	I capitalize characters' names and place names.			

Science Fiction

Peer Review

Read your partner's paper. Then finish each sentence.

1. I see that this science fiction story is organized with _____

_____

_____

_____

2. Some vivid descriptive words that the author uses are _____

_____

_____

_____

3. One detail that the author might include to heighten suspense is _____

_____

_____

_____

Name of Reader _____

Adverbs That Compare

Many **adverbs** can be used to make comparisons. Adverbs can be used to compare the actions of two or more persons, places, or things.

Juanita ran fast.

Jessica ran faster than Juanita.

Noah ran the fastest of all.

Add -*er* to the simple adverb to compare two actions.

Add -*est* to the simple adverb to compare more than two actions.

A Complete the chart below by adding the correct form of the adverb used to compare actions.

Simple adverb	Form to use when comparing two actions	Form to use when comparing more than two actions
quick		
loud		
slow		

B Circle the correct form of the adverb in the parentheses to complete each sentence.

1. Monte climbed (higher, highest) than anyone else.

2. Lisa won the award because she worked (harder, hardest) of all!

3. The Yukon trail stretches (longer, longest) than the Goldmine trail.

4. Last year, Jason grew (taller, tallest) than Mike.

Adverbs That Compare

The words *more* and *most* are often used to form comparisons with adverbs that end in *-ly*.

> Juanita ran quickly.
>
> Jessica ran more quickly than Juanita.
>
> Noah ran the most quickly of all.

Use *more* to compare two actions. Use *most* to compare more than two actions. When you use more and most, do not use the ending *-er* or *-est*.

A Complete the chart below by adding the correct form of the adverb to compare actions.

Adverb	Form to use when comparing two actions	Form to use when comparing more than two actions
easily		
carefully		
clearly		

B Circle the correct form of the adverb in the parentheses to complete each sentence.

1. You can see the farmlands (more clearly, most clearly) from the top of the mountain than on the ground.

2. Yolanda climbed the mountain (more carefully, most carefully) of all!

3. Simon found the trail (more easily, most easily) than I.

Prepositions

A **preposition** links nouns, pronouns and phrases to other words in a sentence.

Prepositions often show place, or where something is located. Look at the box below for some frequently used prepositions.

above	by	over
behind	in	under
below	inside	next to
beside	off	near
between	on	out

A **Circle the preposition in each sentence.**

1. The creek is down the mountain.

2. You might find bears in the forest.

3. The cabin is near the river.

4. The horses are inside the barn.

B **Choose a preposition to correctly complete each sentence.**

1. The pool is _____ the building.

2. The mall is _____ my house.

3. You can see leaves _____ the ground.

4. The cat chased the ball _____ the yard.

Prepositional Phrases

A **prepositional phrase** starts with a preposition and ends with a noun. It includes all the words in between. Experienced writers use prepositional phrases to provide more details in their writing.

We are *near the mountains*.

I see clouds *in the sky*.

The moose are hiding *behind the bushes*.

A Underline the prepositional phrase or phrases in each sentence and circle each preposition.

1. The train raced through the tunnel.

2. Is your umbrella in the closet?

3. Your mother is on the telephone.

4. The boys are under the table.

5. We went to the museum with our class.

B Write a prepositional phrase to complete each sentence.

1. We parked _____

2. The flowers grew _____

3. LaTonya sat _____

4. My dog hides _____

5. We read the newspaper _____

Using Test-Taking Strategies

Read this sample question based on *A Tour of the Western Region*.

Which states listed below are part of the Western region?

Ⓐ Florida, Montana, Idaho, Wyoming
Ⓑ New Mexico, Arizona, Utah, Nevada
Ⓒ Colorado, New York, Ohio, Texas
Ⓓ California, Wyoming, Utah, Idaho

Think carefully about each answer choice:

- Is Ⓐ a possible answer? No, look on page 383. The map does not show Florida as part of the Western States.

- Is Ⓑ a possible answer? The map shows New Mexico, Arizona, Utah, and Nevada in this region.

- Is Ⓒ a possible answer? No, Texas is not in this region.

- Is Ⓓ a possible answer? No, California is not part of the Western States.

By thinking carefully about each answer choice, and checking back to see what the story says, you can pick the correct answer. In this case, B is the answer.

Applying Test-Taking Strategies

Here are more questions to answer. Look carefully at each answer choice. Select the correct answer.

1. Why did many people move to the West more than one hundred years ago?

   Ⓐ It was hot and dry.
   Ⓑ There weren't many people who lived there.
   Ⓒ The people wanted to move.
   Ⓓ The people wanted to find gold.
   (page 385)

2. Why is the Colorado River so important to the region?

   Ⓐ People like to swim in the river.
   Ⓑ It shapes the economy of the area.
   Ⓒ People drink water from the river.
   Ⓓ It helps animals live.
   (page 388)

3. Who were the first people to live in the region?

   Ⓐ The Irish settlers
   Ⓑ The Ancestral Pueblo Native American tribe
   Ⓒ The immigrants from other countries
   Ⓓ The Americans from other states
   (page 392)

My Weekly Planner	
Week of _____	
Theme Vocabulary	This week's words:
Differentiated Vocabulary	This week's words:
Comprehension Strategy and Skill	This week's comprehension strategy: This week's comprehension skill:
Vocabulary Strategy	This week's vocabulary strategy:
Spelling/Word Study Skill	This week's spelling skill:
Word Study Skill	This week's word study skill:
Fluency	This week's fluency selection:
Writing and Language Arts	This week's writing form:
Grammar	This week's grammar skills:

Word Origins

Read about the words from which these English words came. Then write each word beside the explanation it matches.

treasure	fulfill	distress
convenient	exchange	droop

1. This word is from the Old English word *fullfyllan,* meaning "to fill up" or "to make full." The modern English word is defined as "to carry out or finish."

_____

2. This word is from the Old Norse word *drúpa,* meaning "to hang the head." The English word is defined as "to bend or hang down limply."

_____

3. This word is from the Old French word *exchangier,* meaning "barter, or trade one thing for another," and *ex,* meaning "out." The English word is defined as "to give and receive things of the same kind."

_____

4. This word is from the Latin words *con,* meaning "together," and *venire,* meaning "come." The English word is defined as "involving little trouble or effort."

_____

5. This word is from the Greek word *thesauros,* meaning "storehouse." The English word is defined as "to cherish or consider to have great value."

_____

6. This word is from the Latin word *distringere,* meaning "to stretch apart." The English word is defined as "extreme anxiety, sorrow, or pain."

_____

Related Words

Fill in the T-chart below with at least three words related to each vocabulary word.

Vocabulary Word	Related Words
fulfill	
exchange	
treasure	
convenient	
distress	
drooping	

Words with Three Syllables

			Frequently misspelled words	Review words
example	vacation	tomato		
deliver	victory	memory		
important	imagine	president		squirrel
history	remember	favorite	probably	simple
hospital	camera		suddenly	
several	library			

A **Find and circle this week's spelling words in the word snakes below. Then fill in the missing letters for each word in the word list. The first one has been done for you.**

s u d d e n l y k l a v a c a t i o n z
                  s e v e r a l t r e x a m p l e

d e l i v e r o u p r e s i d e n t g c f a v o r i t e l t
     s m e m o r y d   m e s h o s p i t a l s i l

x i m p o r t a n t i h i s t o r y k   t h v i c t o r y q
     s i m a g i n e t e r e m e m b e r r f u d

1. exam*ple*   8. sudd _____
2. fav ___ ite _____   9. ___ spit _____
3. ___ ident _____   10. s ___ al _____
4. mem _____   11. vaca _____
5. ___ iver _____   12. ___ tory _____
6. ___ port _____   13. ima _____
7. his ___ y _____   14. re ___ ber _____

B Proofread the paragraph below. Circle the misspelled words and then rewrite the paragraph on the lines below, using correct spelling, punctuation, and capitalization.

who is your favorite presidant Mine is theodore roosevelt. you can imgine, then, how excited I was when my family went on a vacasion to mount rushmore in august Before we left, I went to the liberry and read the histery of mount rushmore I also reminded my mother sevarel times to remimber to bring the camara. She doesn't have the greatest memery and would probly forget it. i was very relieved when I saw her with it that day because Mount Rushmore was absolutely breathtaking What a marvelous exemple of large-scale sculpture. it was a trip i will never forget

_____

_____

_____

_____

_____

_____

_____

_____

Interview

Practice reading this interview to a partner.

Roaring Downriver

Reported by Will Howard

REPORTER: I'm standing near the winding waters of the Colorado River. The majestic walls of the Grand Canyon are towering overhead. I have with me rafting tour guide Tina Patel. Tina, what can you tell our viewers about rafting?

TINA: White-water rafting is extremely popular in these picturesque mountains; it's exhilarating!

REPORTER: It looks dangerous—is it?

TINA: Not if you follow basic safety rules.

REPORTER: Why is it called "white water," Tina?

TINA: Well, the rapids are so rough that a layer of white foam bubbles above the surface of the water.

REPORTER: What is a white-water raft trip like?

TINA: Oh, rafters will get wet! The water rises up and splashes over the sides of the boat. Sizeable rocks jut up from the water, and the raft swerves to avoid them. Then the fast-moving water drops, and the raft shoots forward. What a thrill!

REPORTER: Have you ever gone over a waterfall?

TINA: Sure, many times. The excitement never ends.

Did you read the interview with fluency? Use the form on the next page to evaluate yourself and your partner.

Reading Response Form

A On a scale of 1 to 5, rate yourself and your partner. Do this for the first reading and final readings, at least. On a scale of 1 to 5, 5 is considered outstanding, 3 is good, and 1 is average.

1. Did I ...

	First Reading	Second Reading	Final Reading
Read the words correctly?			
Read at a good pace?			
Read with expression?			
Read clearly for my audience?			

2. Did my partner ...

	First Reading	Second Reading	Final Reading
Read the words correctly?			
Read at a good pace?			
Read with expression?			
Read clearly for the audience?			

B After the first reading, share with your partner how you thought he or she read, and offer suggestions for improvement.

C After the final reading, answer the following questions for yourself.

1. What did I do well?

First Reading _____

Second Reading _____

Final Reading _____

2. What should I do to improve my reading next time?

First Reading _____

Second Reading _____

Final Reading _____

Make Predictions

Making predictions means making informed guesses about what you are about to read. If you're reading fiction, think about what might happen next. If you're reading nonfiction, think about the kinds of information you might learn. Readers make predictions before reading and to check their understanding while they read.

You work with predictions at all points in your reading—before, during, and after:

Before you read

Look at the title, chapter names, and subheads, illustrations, photos, captions, and other text features to make predictions.

While you read

Use clues from the selection and things you already know to make predictions.

After you read

Stop to check your predictions and revise them if necessary.

Answer the questions below.

1. The title of the story is "Fort Couch, Phoenix, and Popcorn." What

do you think this story will be about? _____

_____

2. Read this passage. Has your prediction changed? If so,
write your new prediction on the lines below the passage.

Jamie and Allison loved Friday nights. They didn't
have to go to school the next day, so they could
stay up later. One of their favorite things do was
to build a couch fort.

_____

_____

3. Read the next passage. Then predict what will happen next.

They took all the cushions off the couch. Then they got the
pillows and all the blankets from their beds.

_____

_____

4. Read on. Then make a prediction about what will happen next.

They stacked all the cushions in front of the couch. Then they
used the blankets to make a roof. They made sure the fort
was big enough for three.

_____

_____

5. Read on. Was your prediction correct?

When their fort was done, they called out for their dog. "Come
here, Phoenix!" All three of them ate popcorn in the fort.

_____

_____

Use Descriptive Language

Authors use **descriptive language** to better describe people, places, and events. Descriptive language helps readers use their five senses to imagine how something looks, sounds, smells, tastes, or feels. Descriptive language includes synonyms, adjectives, and adverbs.

Synonyms are words that have the same meaning or almost the same meaning as another word. In the examples below, the author replaced the word *ran* with the synonym *raced* to add excitement.

- Sergio ran home to tell Mom about the dog.

- Sergio raced home to tell Mom about the dog.

Adjectives describe nouns. Here, the author adds the highlighted adjectives to help the reader "hear" the train.

- The train blew its whistle.

- The train blew its loud, shrill whistle.

Adverbs describe verbs. Adverbs tell how or when something happened. Many adverbs end in -*ly*, but some do not, such as *well*, *after*, and *always*. In the examples below, the author adds the highlighted adverbs to better describe how Tania walked.

- Tania walked out the door.

- Tania walked slowly and quietly out the door.

A Write two synonyms for each word listed in the table below. Then write two adjectives or two adverbs that describe the word. You may use a thesaurus to help you. The first one has been done for you.

Word	Synonyms	Adjectives or Adverbs
run, *v.*	*jog, trot*	*fast, slowly*
jump, *v.*		
call, *v.*		
animal, *n.*		
house, *n.*		
child, *n.*		

B Write a brief story on the lines below. Use at least three of the synonyms, adjectives, or adverbs from the table above.

_____

_____

_____

_____

_____

_____

Before and After Reading

Before you read your Theme Reader, answer these questions. Put a
Y for yes and an *N* for no. Answer them again after you read.

Before reading	Juan Verdades: The Man Who Couldn't Tell a Lie	After reading
	Statement	
	1. Does everybody lie, at least a little?	
	2. Is it easy to get into arguments with your friends over small things?	
	3. Should people be careful of whom they trust?	
	4. Do people often have secret plans that they do not tell anyone else about?	
	5. Should people treasure things more than people?	
	6. Does love make people do things they wouldn't usually do?	
	7. Do people always do the right thing, no matter what?	
	8. Can people use their wits to get out of a sticky situation?	
	9. Is it sometimes better to tell a lie than to tell the truth?	
	10. Is it all right to trick an innocent person to win a bet?	
	11. Is it foolish to risk your home and all your land on one bet?	
	12. Does having confidence sometimes backfire on people?	
	13. Is an honest person better than a smart person?	

Plot, Conflict, and Resolution

Plot is the order of events that happen in a story. In many stories, characters sometimes experience **conflict**. A conflict is a problem or disagreement between characters. The **resolution** is the outcome, or how the conflict ends.

The events in the story below are out of order. In column 1, write the numbers 1 through 10 to show the correct order. In column 3, write a letter C next to the sentences that show conflict, and a letter R next to the sentences that show the resolution.

Numbers	Plot	C or R
	"Everything you do for me means a lot to me. I'm sorry I didn't thank you," said Abby. "I'm sorry I broke your mirror. I'll buy you a new one if you could lend me some money."	
	On the second day of the visit, Abby ran out of clean clothes, so Lizzie did her laundry.	
	Lizzie's mouth dropped open. Then she saw the twinkle in Abby's eye. Abby could always make her laugh.	
	Lizzie got mad. "I gave you money, and I washed your clothes. You never thanked me. And now you've broken my mirror."	
	On the first day of the visit, Abby ran out of money, so Lizzie gave her some.	
	A few days after Abby left, Lizzie got a thank-you card from Abby. "When you come to visit me, I promise I'll do your laundry," it said. "I'll take you up on that," Lizzie said to herself.	
	"I didn't ask you for money or to wash my clothes. You don't have to do things for me," Abby said.	
	Lizzie's friend Abby came to visit her from California.	
	On the third day of the visit, Abby broke Lizzie's hand mirror.	
	"When you stay at my house, you're my guest," said Lizzie. "I'm supposed to do things for you, and you're supposed to thank me. I'm hurt that you don't seem to care."	

Read and Respond

Read the questions. Write your answers on the lines.

1. What do you think of the two men who made the bet? Were they right to put Juan Verdades into an uncomfortable spot?

_____

_____

_____

2. Which character in the story did you relate to the most? Why?

_____

_____

_____

3. How would you describe the character of Juan Verdades? Is he a hero? Why or why not?

_____

_____

_____

4. What would you do if someone tried to trick you into telling a lie?

_____

_____

_____

5. Do you think Juan Verdades, Araceli, and don Arturo will live happily ever after? Why or why not?

_____

_____

_____

Sequence Events

When things happen in a certain order, they are in **sequence**. Events in a story happen in a sequence. Sequencing events helps you understand what you read.

Signal words that tell you the sequence of events are:

first   next   last   before   after   finally

A **Read the passage below. Underline any signal words to help you understand the sequence.**

When I woke up on the first day of vacation I was so excited! I couldn't wait to get to the beach. First, I packed all of the things I would need. After that, we loaded everything into the car and headed to the ocean. Before we could unload the car at the beach, though, Mom made us all put on sunscreen. Next, we went swimming, ate lunch and built a sand castle. After a long day in the sun we headed home. What a great day!

B **In the boxes below, write the sequence of events from the passage. Each event goes in a box.**

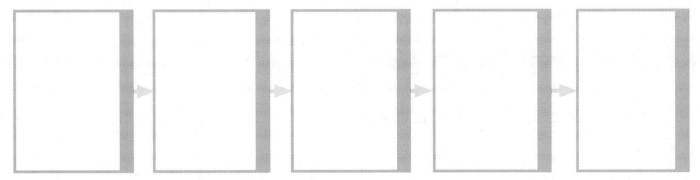

Prefixes

Remember, **prefixes** are word parts placed at the beginning of a word. You can use the meaning of a prefix to help you figure out the meaning of a word.

Prefixes that mean "bad" or "opposite" include:

un-   de-   dis-   counter-   mis-

A **Look at the words below. Circle the prefix.**

1. misplace

2. unhappy

3. defrost

4. disorder

5. counterclockwise

B **Write a sentence for the five words above.**

1. _____

_____

2. _____

_____

3. _____

_____

4. _____

_____

5. _____

_____

Inquiry Checklist: Week 3

Put a check mark next to each item once it is complete.

Share New Information

☐ Each person in my group shared information.

☐ We revised our conjecture if our understandings changed.

☐ We filled in the Idea Tracker for Week 3.

6. Develop Presentation

☐ We chose a format for our presentation.
    PRACTICE COMPANION **200, 373**

☐ We talked about how we might use technology in our presentation.

☐ We created the presentation format.

☐ We used the Presentation Organizer to plan our presentation.

☐ We gave a speaking part to each group member.

☐ All group members completed their Week 3 Inquiry Planners.
    PRACTICE COMPANION **246**

Notes:

_____

_____

_____

_____

_____

_____

_____

_____

_____

Inquiry Planner: Week 3

**Write your group's updated Inquiry Question and your Conjecture.
Then write your Action Plan for next week.**

My group's updated Inquiry Question is: _____

_____

My group's updated conjecture is: _____

_____

Action Plan

1. What topics will I collect information for? _____

_____

_____

2. What sources will I use? _____

_____

_____

3. Where will I find these sources? _____

_____

_____

4. When will I collect information? _____

_____

_____

5. How will I record the information? _____

_____

_____

Focus Question: What is life like in the Mountain States?

What did you learn about life in the Mountain States? Fill in the Web below with your answers.

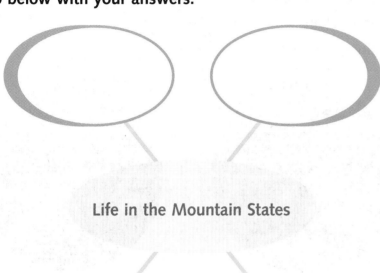

Life in the Mountain States

What makes the West exceptional? Use examples from your selection or your prior knowledge to write your answer on the lines below.

_____

_____

_____

_____

_____

_____

Focus Question: What is life like in the Pacific States?

Think about the following things: *working on a commercial fishing boat; building a new railroad;* and *traveling the Oregon Trail.* How do these experiences help explain life in the Pacific States? Write your answers on the lines below.

Working on a Commercial Fishing Boat

_____

_____

_____

Building a New Railroad

_____

_____

_____

Traveling the Oregon Trail

_____

_____

_____

My Weekly Planner

Week of _____

Theme Vocabulary	This week's words:
Differentiated Vocabulary	This week's words:
Comprehension Strategy and Skill	This week's comprehension strategy: This week's comprehension skill:
Vocabulary Strategy	This week's vocabulary strategy:
Spelling/Word Study Skill	This week's spelling skill:
Word Study Skill	This week's word study skill:
Fluency	This week's fluency selection:
Writing and Language Arts	This week's writing form:
Grammar	This week's grammar skills:

Connect Vocabulary

Write sentences using the two vocabulary words given. You may use any form of the words in any order.

1. missionary, fulfill _____

_____

2. rugged, extremes _____

_____

3. arid, irrigated _____

_____

4. film, treasure _____

_____

5. exchange, missionary _____

_____

6. fulfill, film _____

_____

7. arid, extremes _____

_____

Relate Vocabulary

Use the words in the word bank to answer the questions.

arid	irrigated	extremes
missionary	fulfill	treasure
rugged	exchange	film

1. Which word means the opposite of rainy?

_____

2. Which word is related to preach?

_____

3. Which word means the same as satisfy?

_____

4. Which word has a similar meaning to the word value?

_____

5. Which word is related to farming?

_____

6. Which word means the opposite of smooth?

_____

7. Which word is related to photography?

_____

8. Which word is related to unusual?

_____

9. Which word has a similar meaning to the word trade?

_____

Words with Silent Consonants

			Frequently misspelled words	Review words
half	answer	climb		
comb	handsome	honest		remember
calm	knuckle	limb	eighth	hospital
often	wrinkle	plumber	know	
honor	yolk			
listen	folktale			

A Say each spelling word. Circle the silent consonant or consonants.

1. k n u c k l e

2. h a l f

3. h a n d s o m e

4. c o m b

5. w r i n k l e

6. k n o w

7. c a l m

8. o f t e n

9. y o l k

10. e i g h t h

11. h o n o r

12. f o l k t a l e

13. c l i m b

14. h o n e s t

15. l i s t e n

B Proofread the paragraph below and circle the misspelled words. Write the correct spelling of each word on the lines.

The onest plumer ofen took long walks during his lunch break. His walks were a tradition that he onored every day. He would clime to the top of a hill and enjoy the cam breezes and beautiful view of the valley. The scene reminded him of the settings in many foketales that he had read. The tree lims swayed in the breeze and he would lisen to the birds chirping. He would anser their chirps by whistling at them. After a haf hour or so, he would walk back down the hill and return to work.

1. _____
2. _____
3. _____
4. _____
5. _____
6. _____
7. _____
8. _____
9. _____
10. _____
11. _____

Journal Entry

Practice reading this journal entry to a partner.

At the Trail's End

by Jonathan White

Dear Journal,

We have lived on the coast of Oregon for several years now. We traveled many miles along the Oregon Trail and then continued our journey to the sea. Father was determined to see the ocean. It was very difficult, but we are happy in our new home. The land here is so different from the plains we left behind! There are huge mountains and stunning lakes, but most stunning is the Pacific Ocean. It stretches as far as I can see. When huge waves crash against the rocky coast, I feel small and insignificant. I am in awe of the power that it unleashes.

With all this water around us, my family has become fishers. We catch numerous types of fish and sell them in town. My whole family likes fishing much more than we liked farming.

It gets frigid here in the winter, and cold weather lasts much longer than it did on the plains. The first winter was especially rough, but we all made it through. All in all, life here has been good to us. Starting a new life in the Pacific Northwest was a perfect move for my family.

Did you read the journal entry with fluency? Use the form on the next page to evaluate yourself and your partner.

Reading Response Form

A On a scale of 1 to 5, rate yourself and your partner. Do this for the first reading and final readings, at least. On a scale of 1 to 5, 5 is considered outstanding, 3 is good, and 1 is average.

1. Did I ...

	First Reading	Second Reading	Final Reading
Read the words correctly?			
Read at a good pace?			
Read with expression?			
Read clearly for my audience?			

2. Did my partner ...

	First Reading	Second Reading	Final Reading
Read the words correctly?			
Read at a good pace?			
Read with expression?			
Read clearly for the audience?			

B After the first reading, share with your partner how you thought he or she read, and offer suggestions for improvement.

C After the final reading, answer the following questions for yourself.

1. What did I do well?

First Reading _____

Second Reading _____

Final Reading _____

2. What should I do to improve my reading next time?

First Reading _____

Second Reading _____

Final Reading _____

Determine Important Information

When you **determine important information** you find the key ideas in the selection. Separating the key ideas from the smaller details will help you understand the important information. Look for clues to help you recognize the important information the author wants you to know.

Tip 1 Look for key words. Key words may be:
- In the title, chapter names, or subheads
- **Boldface** or highlighted
- Repeated in many parts of the selection

Tip 2 Look at the text features. They could provide clues to the important information in the selection.

Tips for determining important information

Tip 3 Carefully read the first and last sentences in each paragraph. Authors often put important information here.

Tip 4 Stop after each section and ask questions.
- What is the most important idea of this section?
- Can I pick out a sentence that tells the most important idea?
- Which information is interesting but not that important?

Read the passage. Then answer the questions.

Thousands of soldiers and hundreds of horses, all made of terra-cotta (a kind of clay) and buried in the ground—what could this be? It's the terra-cotta army, and it was buried with a Chinese emperor about 2,200 years ago. A group of farmers digging a well discovered the army in 1974. Many of the statues were broken, but some have been reassembled.

The army is life-sized. This big clay army was meant to protect the emperor in the afterlife. One amazing thing about the soldiers is that they all have different faces, just like real people. This means that workers had to make all the faces by hand. They used a mold and then formed the features with extra clay.

1. What information in the passage would probably be most important to an artist? _____

_____

2. What is the most important information in the first paragraph? _____

_____

3. What is the least important information in the first paragraph? _____

_____

4. Which sentence in the second paragraph is not important for picturing what the statues looked like? _____

_____

Use Multiple Strategies

Now you have three more vocabulary strategies in your reading toolbox: synonyms, context clues, and descriptive language.

See the Word Map below for a quick review of these strategies.

Synonym:
A synonym is a word that has the same or almost the same meaning as another word. Synonyms are useful for both reading and writing. You can use synonyms to help you understand unfamiliar words. You can also use synonyms to make your writing more interesting. You can find synonyms for a word in the dictionary or a thesaurus.

Context clues:
Context clues are words in a text that help you understand the meaning of an unfamiliar word. Some context clues give the meaning of the word. Sometimes a context clue is another word or phrase located next to the word. Some context clues are synonyms or antonyms.

Vocabulary Strategies

Descriptive language:
Descriptive language consists of words that help readers use their five senses to imagine how something looks, sounds, smells, tastes, or feels. Authors use descriptive language to better describe people, places, and events. Descriptive language includes synonyms, adjectives, and adverbs.

Read the passage. Then answer the questions.

What do you do when you get tickled? You laugh. Guess what? So do gorillas, chimps, orangutans, and slender chimp-like apes called bonobos. Scientists have recently discovered that the fast panting, grunts, and quick snorts that ape youngsters make while being tickled is laughter. Scientists have also learned that chimps laugh while both breathing out and breathing in. It sounds like noisy breathing. Gorillas and bonobos—and humans—laugh only by breathing out. Unlike ape laughter, happy human giggling sounds pretty. This is because the vibrations, or back-and-forth movements, of our vocal cords can make our laughter sound like the lovely tones from a musical instrument.

1. What context clue helps you understand what a bonobo is? _____

_____

2. What context clue explains the meaning of the word *vibrations*? _____

_____

3. Write two words from the passage that are synonyms that both mean

sounds you make while being tickled. _____

4. What category do the words *bonobo, chimp,* and *gorilla* belong to? _____

_____

5. Circle three phrases that help you use your sense of hearing.

6. Which words are synonyms for "find out"? _____

_____

Before and After Reading

Before you read the next selection, read these statements and put a check next to the ones you believe to be true. Check again after reading.

Before reading	Onward to Oregon! Statement	After reading
	1. Smokestack Rock is a landmark on the Missouri Trail.	
	2. Cholera is a deadly disease that sometimes struck pioneers heading westward.	
	3. One of the routes west for wagon trains was called the Pacific Trail.	
	4. Wagon trains stopped for supplies at Independence Rock.	

Before reading	Deckhands Statement	After reading
	1. Ketchikan, Alaska, is known for its tuna fishing.	
	2. The summer days in Alaska are very long because Alaska is so far north.	
	3. A salmon run is when large schools of salmon return from the ocean to the rivers to mate.	
	4. Alaskans call the continental United States the Bigger Forty-Eight.	

Mink and the Sun

Before reading	Statement	After reading
	1. It is natural for someone who is different to be teased by other people.	
	2. Everyone is born to fulfill a special purpose in life.	
	3. Even people with important jobs to do need the support of their family and friends.	
	4. If you're strong and you know who you are, you don't have to answer to anyone.	

The Mystery of the Railroad Letters

Before reading	Statement	After reading
	1. The telegram was a way to send messages with clicks.	
	2. Towns that have a railroad stop usually grow and prosper.	
	3. Northern Pacific was the name of a highway line in the Pacific Northwest.	
	4. Tacoma was the end, or terminus, of the Transcontinental Railroad.	

Recall and Retell

When you **recall**, you tell the most important details and events.

When you **retell** something, you describe what happened in a selection.

Read the passage below.

In the Western State of Idaho, you will see many potato farms. The soil in Idaho makes it perfect for growing potatoes. The land is irrigated by water being carried to it by pipes and ditches. The water keeps the soil very moist and rich for growing potatoes. The next time you visit the grocery store, look at the potatoes. Chances are, you will find all colors and shapes of potatoes grown in Idaho.

Use your own words to recall and retell the information in the passage. Write your ideas in the boxes below.

Contractions

Remember, a **contraction** is a short way to write two words together. You use an apostrophe (') to replace some of the letters.

would not = wouldn't

would have = would've

cannot = can't

A Write a contraction on the line for the words below.

1. you would = _____

2. they have= _____

3. is not = _____

4. will not = _____

B Write a sentence for each contraction from Part A.

1. _____

_____

2. _____

_____

3. _____

_____

4. _____

_____

Inquiry Checklist: Week 4

Put a check mark next to each item once it is complete.

Share New Information

☐ Each person in my group shared information.

☐ We revised our conjecture if our understandings changed.

7. Deliver Presentation

☐ We rehearsed our presentation.

☐ We presented for another group.

☐ We used the Presentation Rubric to evaluate our own presentation.

☐ We used the Presentation Rubric to evaluate the other group's presentation.

☐ We received feedback. We used the Presentation Organizer to revise our presentation.

Identify New Questions

☐ All group members listed new questions on their Week 4 Inquiry Planners.
PRACTICE COMPANION **265**

☐ We posted new questions on the Question Board.

Notes:

_____

_____

_____

_____

_____

_____

_____

Inquiry Planner: Week 4

Write your new questions and your plans for finding out more.

1. What other questions do I have? _____

_____

_____

_____

2. What sources can I use to find out more? _____

_____

_____

_____

3. Where will I find these sources? _____

_____

_____

_____

4. When will I collect information? _____

_____

_____

_____

Self-Assessment Rubric

Read each goal in the chart. Make a check mark to give yourself a score of 3, 2, or 1. Then finish the sentences below.

Category	Goals	Very Good 3	OK 2	Needs Work 1
Group Role	I understood and fulfilled my role.			
Participation	I helped my group do each step of the Inquiry Process.			
Research	I did research on my own and shared it with my group.			
Listening	I gave others a chance to speak and listened well.			
Collaboration	I shared my ideas and respected others' ideas.			
Responsibility	I stayed on task during group work.			
Presentation	I was prepared for our presentation. I spoke clearly and effectively.			
Enjoyment	I enjoyed working with others in my group.			

1. One thing I did well was _____

_____

2. One thing I would like to do better is _____

_____

What did your selection tell you about life in the Pacific States? Fill in the Web below with details that describe life in the Pacific States.

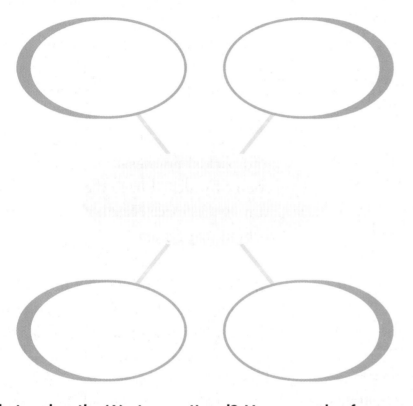

What makes the West exceptional? Use examples from your selection or your prior knowledge to answer the question on the lines below.

_____

_____

_____

_____

_____

_____

_____

Study the Model

Autobiography

Read the Writing Model along with your teacher. Look for the time order of events as well as the sensory words.

Life in a Small Town

by Mimi Theriault

When I was very small, I lived with my parents in Seattle, Washington. My mother was an engineer for a company that made airplanes. We had an apartment in the middle of downtown, where life rushed around us. I used to love standing by the window to watch people, dogs, and cars pass. Every weekend, we went to Pike Place Market to buy fresh vegetables, and I listened to street musicians and watched boats on the water.

I loved Seattle, but my parents weren't happy there. My mom worked long hours at her job—sometimes she didn't get home until midnight. Then she worked from home on weekends. She always said there weren't enough hours in the day.

One day, my parents announced that we were moving to a small town in Alaska. I couldn't believe it! I was sure I would hate our new town.

I said good-bye to my friends and packed up everything in my room. I watched from the moving van as the Space Needle disappeared behind me. I cried.

Now I have lived in Yakutat for two years. Life here is very different. My mom still works with airplanes, but now she works in a tiny airport and has plenty of time off. Our house still sits near the coast, but the waterfront isn't crowded like it was in Seattle. On weekends, instead of going to a big market, we go fishing or hiking. Sometimes I miss Seattle, but I feel more at home in Alaska every day.

Evaluation Rubric

Autobiography

Writing Traits	Goals	Yes	Needs Work!	Now it's OK.
Organization	My autobiography has a beginning, a middle, and an end.			
	I put my events in a logical sequence.			
Ideas	I talk about an exact time in my life that was important to me.			
	I include an introduction that will grab readers' attention.			
Voice	I use first-person point of view.			
	My personality shows in my writing.			
Word Choice	I use the right shade of meaning for each word.			
	I use descriptive language.			
Sentence Fluency	I use transition words between paragraphs.			
	I use time order words.			
Conventions	I avoid double negatives.			
	I use correct punctuation.			
	I use the right spelling for troublesome word groups.			
	All the words are spelled correctly.			

Autobiography

Peer Review

Read your partner's paper. Then finish each sentence.

1. I see that this autobiography is organized with _____

_____

_____

_____

2. Some good descriptive words or phrases that the author uses are _____

_____

_____

_____

3. One example of a transition word that the author might use is _____

_____

_____

_____

Name of Reader_____

Prepositions

Remember, a **preposition** links nouns, pronouns and phrases to other words in a sentence.

Prepositions often show position, or where something is located. Common prepositions are listed below.

above   near   behind   on   below
beside   off   over   under   out   in

A **Circle the preposition in each sentence.**

1. The school is down the street.

2. You can sit beside the teacher.

3. The dogs are behind the fence.

4. Put the book on the table.

B **Choose a preposition to correctly complete each sentence.**

1. My sister is hiding _____ the bed.

2. Can you jump _____ the water puddle?

3. Move the trash _____ the counter.

4. The kids ran _____ the playground.

Prepositional Phrases

Remember, a **prepositional phrase** starts with a preposition and ends with a noun. It includes all the words in between. You should use prepositional phrases to provide more details about your writing.

We are swimming *in the ocean.*

Can you jump *over the waves?*

The shells are *in the sand.*

A Underline the prepositional phrase. Circle the preposition.

1. We had a picnic in the park.

2. Get your lunch out of the basket.

3. Your friends are near the playground.

4. The boys are on the slide.

B On the lines below write four sentences that use prepositional phrases.

1. _____

_____

2. _____

_____

3. _____

_____

4. _____

_____

Avoid Double Negatives

The words below are considered negatives. You can only use one negative word in a sentence.

no   none   nothing   neither   not   hardly   nowhere   nobody

If you have two negatives, it is called a double negative. You should always avoid using double negatives in your writing and speaking.

I don't want nothing. — should be ➤ I don't want anything.

We could not find nowhere to play. — should be ➤ We could not find anywhere to play.

Complete the sentences below using the correct word in parentheses.

1. She couldn't eat _____.
(anything, nothing)

2. I didn't leave _____.
(nothing, anything)

3. We hardly had _____ recess time.
(any, no)

4. I can't find my shoes _____.
(nowhere, anywhere)

5. We don't have _____ time to waste.
(no, any)

6. She didn't want to ask _____ for help.
(anybody, nobody)

7. Max didn't go _____ for spring recess.
(nowhere, anywhere)

8. I can't do _____ after school today.
(anything, nothing)

Troublesome Words

Some words sound alike but have different meanings and are spelled differently. When writing, make sure you use the correct form of a word so your ideas make sense to your readers.

Troublesome Words

to, too, two

sit, set

there, they're, their

lay, lie

Underline each correct word in parentheses.

1. I have (to, too, two) friends coming over to play.

2. Please (sit, set) my book on the floor.

3. We are going to (there, they're, their) class to watch a movie.

4. I'm going upstairs to (lay, lie) down and rest.

5. We are going on the bus (to, too, two).

6. You can play over (there, their, they're).

7. We will go (to, too, two) the movies.

8. He will (lay, lie) a blanket on the floor and go to sleep.

Using Test-Taking Strategies

All tests are not the same. Instead of selecting an answer from a list of choices, you might be asked to write your own answer. Here is a sample question based on *Juan Verdades*.

Sample Question:
What happens after don Arturo tells his wife about the bet?

Look carefully at what the question asks you to do:

- You must describe what happens after don Arturo tells his wife about the bet.

- You must give information to support, or back up, your answer.

There are different ways to answer this question. Here are some possible answers:

- Don Arturo's wife begins to cry. But his daughter comes up with a plan. Araceli suggests they stay at don Ignacio's house for the next two weeks.

- Araceli tells her father, don Arturo, they should stay at the Ignacios' ranch for two weeks so they can't lose the bet.

When you write your own answer, check it carefully. Be sure that you do everything the question asks you to do.

Applying Test-Taking Strategies

Now read the question below. Read carefully in order to understand what the question asks you to do.

> Explain why Araceli keeps trying to convince Juan to give her the apples from the tree.

Use the information from *Juan Verdades* to complete the chart. Then use the chart to answer the test question.

Clue from *Juan Verdades*	What I Already Know	My Conclusion
Araceli wants her father to win the bet.	People will do anything to help their family members.	Araceli knows that if she can get Juan to give her the fruit, her father will win.

Use the ideas in the chart to write your answer to the question at the top of the page. Write your answer on a separate sheet of paper.

My Weekly Planner

Week of _____

Theme Vocabulary	This week's words:
Differentiated Vocabulary	This week's words:
Comprehension Strategy and Skill	This week's comprehension strategy: This week's comprehension skill:
Vocabulary Strategy	This week's vocabulary strategy:
Spelling/Word Study Skill	This week's spelling skill:
Word Study Skill	This week's word study skill:
Fluency	This week's fluency selection:
Writing and Language Arts	This week's writing form:
Grammar	This week's grammar skills:

Identify Examples

List three words from the word bank below that are examples of each vocabulary word.

dreams	practice	love
exercise	money	climb
fame	hunger	trophy

1. motivation: the influence or the reason that makes a person do something (Hint: Think of things that might push a person to act.)

_____

_____

_____

2. goal: a purpose or something a person wants to achieve (Hint: Think about things a person might want.)

_____

_____

_____

3. strive: to try very hard or make a great effort (Hint: Think about action words that describe a person doing something that takes effort.)

_____

_____

_____

Related Words

For each vocabulary word, write four related words in the chart below. Think of one noun, one verb, one adjective, and one adverb. You may use a dictionary or thesaurus to help you.

Related Words

goal

Noun:

Verb:

Adjective:

Adverb:

motivation

Noun:

Verb:

Adjective:

Adverb:

strive

Noun:

Verb:

Adjective:

Adverb:

symbol

Noun:

Verb:

Adjective:

Adverb:

Words Ending in *-tion*, *-ture*, and *-ure*

attention	caution	failure	**Frequently misspelled words**	**Review words**
fraction	culture	mixture		folktale
fiction	creature	pressure	happened	often
mention	nature	injure	might	
caption	future			
station	measure			

A Read each spelling word and listen for the sound you hear at the end of the word. Write each spelling word in the correct column. The first one has been done for you.

-tion	-ture	-ure
caption		

B Proofread the paragraph. Rewrite the paragraph on the lines below, correcting the spelling, punctuation, and capitalization errors.

You will never guess what hapned on my natur walk yesterday. my sister and I saw this strange creture! It caught our atention right away. it had bright green skin and very long legs. I knew we had to use cation if we got close to it The animal mght be dangerous. It could even ijure us. What was this creature Could it be found in another cultur It reminded me of something you would read about in a fictn story. My sister and I moved forward very slowly. The creature didn't seem to be moving. My sister was brave enough to go even closer. Suddenly, she started laughing and said, "Maria, it is only a plastic tree frog!"

_____

_____

_____

_____

_____

_____

_____

_____

_____

Fable

Practice reading this fable to a partner.

Armadillo's Song

A Bolivian fable retold by Juan Cortez

Once there was an armadillo who loved to listen to music. He especially enjoyed hearing the frogs frolic and sing as they jumped about the pond. Armadillo watched them every day and sighed aloud, "If only I could sing!"

One day noisy crickets crowded around the pond. Armadillo heard them chirping and singing, and he sighed aloud again, "If only I could sing!"

A family of yellow canaries nested in a tree near Armadillo's house. Their lovely melodies drifted through the air. Jealous Armadillo sighed aloud once more, "If only I could sing!"

Finally Armadillo could take it no longer. He told a wizard how dearly he wanted to be able to sing. The wizard thought for a moment and then said, "I can make you sing, but in exchange I will have to take your shell."

Armadillo said he would do anything to be able to sing. So the wizard took his shell, and it became the finest musical instrument around. The shell made enchanting music, and all who listened cheered, "Armadillo has learned to sing at last!"

Moral: Artists often make sacrifices for their art.

Did you read the fable with fluency? Use the form on the next page to evaluate yourself and your partner.

Reading Response Form

A On a scale of 1 to 5, rate yourself and your partner. Do this for the first reading and final readings, at least. On a scale of 1 to 5, 5 is considered outstanding, 3 is good, and 1 is average.

1. Did I …

	First Reading	Second Reading	Final Reading
Read the words correctly?			
Read at a good pace?			
Read with expression?			
Read clearly for my audience?			

2. Did my partner …

	First Reading	Second Reading	Final Reading
Read the words correctly?			
Read at a good pace?			
Read with expression?			
Read clearly for the audience?			

B After the first reading, share with your partner how you thought he or she read, and offer suggestions for improvement.

C After the final reading, answer the following questions for yourself.

1. What did I do well?

First Reading _____

Second Reading _____

Final Reading _____

2. What should I do to improve my reading next time?

First Reading _____

Second Reading _____

Final Reading _____

Make Inferences

When you **make inferences,** you use what you know to fill in information that is not stated in a selection. You can use inferences to better understand a text and answer questions about it. To make inferences, ask yourself what information is missing from a text. Then think about your own experiences and other texts you've read to help you answer these questions.

Read the selection below and see how the student makes an inference to answer the question that follows.

> Michael was so excited. When the last bell rang, he dashed for the door and ran all the way home from school. Today his new skateboard was arriving. It was a custom design that had taken six weeks to make. Today was the day that the board would be waiting for him when he got home.
>
> As Michael ran up the walkway to his house, his mother opened the door. She looked concerned. Michael stopped in his tracks. His heart sank.
>
> "There's been a delay," Michael's mother said. "I'm so sorry, honey."

How do you think Michael's mother feels about him at this moment?

What I read	What I know	Inference
Michael's mother looks concerned. She tells him she is sorry.	My mother feels bad for me when I'm disappointed about something.	Michael's mother feels bad for him.

Complete the chart to make inferences.

What I read	What I know	Inference
Murals are large paintings that are created on walls or ceilings.		
People have been making murals since prehistoric times. Prehistoric murals often showed hunting scenes.		
About 3,500 years ago, people learned how to paint murals on wet plaster on walls. This type of mural is called a fresco.		
Another way of making a mural is mosaic. In mosaic, pieces of colored tile are applied to a wall or ceiling to create a picture.		

Antonyms

An **antonym** is a word whose meaning is the opposite of that of another word. Antonyms can help you understand what you read and help you improve your own writing. You can use a thesaurus and sometimes a dictionary to find antonyms for a word.

When you read an unfamiliar word, you may be able to use an antonym as a context clue. An antonym that is familiar may help you understand the new word. Look for clue words such as *not* or *but* to signal antonyms. In the example below, the word *useful* is an antonym for the word *insignificant*.

- The map was **insignificant**. It was not at all useful in finding the buried treasure.

Sometimes writers use antonyms to make their writing clearer or more interesting. You can add antonyms to your writing in the same way. In the example below, the writer uses the highlighted antonyms of the word *beautiful* to better describe the appearance of the cat.

- My grandmother's cat is beautiful, quite the opposite of this mangy, scruffy stray.

Now look at the words below. Study the antonyms given by the student and try to think of other words that could be antonyms.

1. excited *calm, peaceful, bored*

2. increase *decrease, shrink, reduce*

3. clumsy *graceful, lithe, skillful*

4. bold *meek, timid, shy*

A **Write the word from each sentence that is an antonym for the highlighted word.**

1. Grandma couldn't imagine anything more modern than a push-button phone, but it seemed very old-fashioned to me.

   _____

2. The seals bellowed loudly on the rocks, while the waves lapped softly on the shore. _____

3. Bubba liked warm, mushy oatmeal for breakfast, so when he was served crunchy, cold cereal he had to try really hard not to pout. _____

4. Silvio's desk was orderly, but his file cabinet was really disorganized. _____

B **For each word below, write one or two sentences. Include the word shown and an antonym for the word.**

1. often _____

   _____

2. hate _____

   _____

3. carefully _____

   _____

4. confident _____

   _____

Draw Conclusions

Authors don't always tell you everything you need to know in a selection. As a result, you have to use clues from the selection and what you already know in order to **draw conclusions**.

Read the passage below.

Jake sat in the window. He was looking at a small bird outside. The bird kept singing and jumping around in the plants. This jumping and singing made the end of Jake's tail twist and turn. The rest of his tail wasn't moving at all. Jake would have jumped right out with the bird if the window wasn't in his way.

Complete the chart below. Use clues from the passage and what you already know to draw conclusions about what type of animal Jake is.

Clue from the Passage	What I Already Know	My Conclusion

Adverb Suffixes

Adverbs are words that describe how, when, or where an action takes place. Suffixes are word parts added to the end of a word. Some adverb suffixes you might see include:

-ly   *-ways*   *-wise*

Circle the adverb in each sentence. Underline the suffix.

1. The boys rode their bikes quickly through the park.

2. She stepped sideways to let me pass.

3. The dogs bark loudly at night.

4. The principal stood up, and everyone else did likewise.

5. It rarely snows in Florida.

6. The legs are too long, but otherwise the pants fit.

7. Please walk carefully down the stairs.

8. I finally read that book you gave me last month.

9. We talked quietly in the classroom.

10. The team thoughtfully devised a plan to win the game.

Inquiry Checklist: Week 1

Put a check mark next to each item once it is complete.

Discussion Roles

☐ I took a role in my group.

PRACTICE COMPANION **370**

My role is _____.

---

1. Generate Ideas and Questions

☐ We thought of at least three possible questions.

☐ We chose an Inquiry Question to investigate.

---

2. Make a Conjecture

☐ We shared what we know about our Inquiry Question.

☐ We made a conjecture about our Inquiry Question.

☐ We filled in the Idea Tracker for Week 1.

☐ We put our Inquiry Question and conjecture on the Question Board.

---

3. Make Plans to Collect Information

☐ We made a list of topics to research and split them up among the group.

☐ We used the Information Finder and made a list of possible sources we could use.

PRACTICE COMPANION **371**

☐ All group members completed their Week 1 Inquiry Planners.

PRACTICE COMPANION **291**

Notes:

_____

_____

_____

Inquiry Planner: Week 1

Write your group's Inquiry Question and conjecture. Then write your Action Plan for next week.

My group's Inquiry Question is: _____

_____

My group's conjecture is: _____

_____

Action Plan

1. What topics will I collect information for? _____

    _____

    _____

2. What sources will I use? _____

    _____

    _____

3. Where will I find these sources? _____

    _____

    _____

4. When will I collect information? _____

    _____

    _____

5. How will I record the information? _____

    _____

    _____

Panel Discussion

Read about panel discussions and study the example.

What is a panel discussion?

- A panel discussion is a structured conversation about a topic held in front of an audience.

- A panel that is knowledgeable about a topic sits in front of an audience.

- The audience listens and may ask questions.

- Panel members may also ask each other questions to show different points of view about a topic.

This panel is discussing the importance of working together to stop global warming.

You Can Use Technology

Find out how technology can help you create and share your presentation.

- Log on to **www.wgLEAD21.com.**

- From My Home Page, click on Inquiry Project.

Focus Question: What things do people strive for?

Think about the goals you read about in your selection. What things do people strive for? Why are these things important? Use examples from your selection to fill in the chart below with your answers.

Things People Strive For	Why They Are Important

How do people set and meet goals? Use examples from your selection to explain on the lines below.

_____

_____

_____

_____

_____

_____

_____

_____

_____

Focus Question: What kinds of challenges do people face when working toward their goals?

Think about the following: *setting a personal goal*; *being challenged in meeting your goal*; and *learning how to face that challenge*. How do these things help you work toward your goal? **Write your answers below.**

Setting a personal goal

_____

_____

_____

Being challenged in meeting your goal

_____

_____

_____

Learning how to face the challenge

_____

_____

_____

My Weekly Planner

Week of _____

Theme Vocabulary	This week's words:
Differentiated Vocabulary	This week's words:
Comprehension Strategy and Skill	This week's comprehension strategy: This week's comprehension skill:
Vocabulary Strategy	This week's vocabulary strategy:
Spelling/Word Study Skill	This week's spelling skill:
Word Study Skill	This week's word study skill:
Fluency	This week's fluency selection:
Writing and Language Arts	This week's writing form:
Grammar	This week's grammar skills:

Word Mapping

Fill in a word map for each of the vocabulary words.

1.

Definition

Examples

risk

Non-Examples

Sentence

2.

Definition

Examples

reward

Non-Examples

Sentence

Brainstorm Related Words

For each brainstorming chart below, list six words that are closely related to the vocabulary word at the top. When you have completed your charts, exchange them with a partner and discuss your choices.

	risk	

	flee	

	reward	

Words from Other Languages

			Frequently misspelled words	Review words
salsa	squash	patio		
vanilla	potato	banjo		fraction
ballet	tortilla	pajamas	already	nature
petite	tornado	safari		
studio	noodle		dollar	
skunk	bagel			

A Find the eighteen spelling words hidden in the puzzle.

```
S  A  L  S  A  B  E  A  R  P  S  P  R  A
B  A  R  O  G  A  S  L  O  A  T  O  I  L
Y  A  F  A  H  N  K  R  V  T  U  T  D  R
T  E  L  A  M  J  U  C  D  I  D  A  D  E
V  O  U  L  R  O  N  E  L  O  I  T  L  A
A  N  R  G  E  I  K  A  N  K  O  O  E  D
N  Y  O  T  T  T  R  D  O  L  L  A  R  Y
I  D  D  O  I  S  T  O  R  N  A  D  O  A
L  I  N  J  D  L  P  A  J  A  M  A  S  R
L  W  P  L  E  L  L  B  A  G  E  L  L  V
A  P  E  T  I  T  E  A  S  Q  U  A  S  H
```

B Proofread the paragraph. Rewrite the paragraph on the lines below, correcting the spelling, punctuation, and capitalization errors.

There is an amazing new supermarket in my town My grandmother and I sampled some slsa on a bagl. We found fresh sqash in the produce department. I wanted to try the potat tortila but the line was too long. my grandmother liked the chicken nodle soup so much, she decided to buy some for dinner. She said there was a beautiful ptio where we could eat after we finished shopping. I had a ten dolr bill to spend on something special I wanted to buy some vnilla ice cream. But, I alrdy ate ice cream at lunch. What would I buy I saw a cool sknk toy that made noises, a real bnjo, a trndo experiment, and a sfri game. I couldn't decide how to spend my money, so I decided to save it for my next trip to this great store!

Procedural Text

Practice reading these directions to a partner.

Reach Your Goal!

by Lindsay Lee

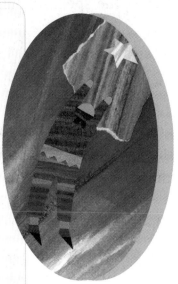

Is there something you want to accomplish? Are you working toward a specific goal? Before you can reach any goal, you need to have a plan.

1. State your goal: Write down as clearly as possible what you want to achieve. Be specific!

2. Create a time line: Choose an end date for achieving your goal. Setting a time limit will help keep you on task. Then select milestone dates along the way.

3. Gather resources: Make a list of all of the things you will need to accomplish your goal. This can include materials, people, books, or Web sites.

4. Write an action plan: Create a plan to follow. Include details about what you need to do and how you will complete each step.

5. Stay on track: Think of ways to stay on schedule as you move forward with your plan. At each milestone, reward yourself for your progress. For example, invite some friends over to celebrate what you have accomplished so far.

6. Taste success: Keep your eyes on the goal, stick to your plan, and follow through. You can do it!

Did you read the directions with fluency? Use the form on the next page to evaluate yourself and your partner.

Reading Response Form

A On a scale of 1 to 5, rate yourself and your partner. Do this for the first reading and final reading, at least. On a scale of 1 to 5, 5 is considered outstanding, 3 is good, and 1 is average.

1. Did I …

	First Reading	Second Reading	Final Reading
Read the words correctly?			
Read at a good pace?			
Read with expression?			
Read clearly for my audience?			

2. Did my partner …

	First Reading	Second Reading	Final Reading
Read the words correctly?			
Read at a good pace?			
Read with expression?			
Read clearly for the audience?			

B After the first reading, share with your partner how you thought he or she read, and offer suggestions for improvement.

C After the final reading, answer the following questions for yourself.

1. What did I do well?

First Reading _____

Second Reading _____

Final Reading _____

2. What should I do to improve my reading next time?

First Reading _____

Second Reading _____

Final Reading _____

Summarize

When you **summarize**, you use your own words to tell the most important ideas of a selection. Summarizing helps you understand and remember what you've read. To summarize a text, list the most important information. Then write the big idea in your own words.

Read the selection below. Then look at how a student summarized the information in a summary chart.

Jacques-Yves Cousteau was a pioneer of underwater exploration. Cousteau was born in France in 1910, and from a young age he loved the sea. In 1942, he helped invent the Aqua-Lung, one of the first underwater breathing devices. Later Cousteau became an oceanographer, a person who studies the seas. From his boat *Calypso*, Cousteau and his crew collected ocean creatures and took underwater photographs.

Cousteau became most famous for his television shows. "The Undersea World of Jacques Cousteau" brought the mysteries of the oceans into the living rooms of people around the world.

Important Idea	**Important Idea**	**Important Idea**
Jacques-Yves Cousteau helped invent the Aqua-Lung.	Cousteau studied the oceans from his research boat.	Cousteau had a television show about the ocean.

Summary:
Jacques-Yves Cousteau was a famous underwater explorer who taught many people about the ocean through his research and television shows.

Read the selection below. Then summarize the selection using the chart.

Arbor Day is a special day set aside for people to plant trees. J. Sterling Morton of Nebraska City, Nebraska, organized the first Arbor Day in 1872. Within 50 years, every state in the United States had an official Arbor Day celebration. The idea of Arbor Day became popular around the world, and now many countries celebrate Arbor Day.

People plant trees on Arbor Day for many reasons. They plant them to make their surroundings more beautiful and to replace trees that have died or been cut down. Some people plant trees to remember loved ones who have passed away. Another good reason to plant trees is to fight global warming.

Important Idea	**Important Idea**	**Important Idea**

Summary:

The big idea of the selection is _____

_____

Analogies

An **analogy** is a statement that compares two things that have something in common. Analogies show relationships between words. The chart below shows several types of analogies.

Synonyms,
such as shout/yell

Antonyms,
such as big/small

Types of analogies

Part to whole,
such as inches/foot

Object to function,
such as phone/talk

Categories,
such as cereal/eggs/toast

You can use analogies as a vocabulary strategy to figure out the meaning of the word *abrupt*.

"Don't let Uncle Drake's coarse manners fool you," Mom said. "He may seem rude on the outside, but he's kind and patient underneath."

The passage uses the synonyms kind and patient and an antonym to those words, rude. It also uses the antonyms outside and underneath. Manners are something that people show on the outside. So if Uncle Drake seems rude on the outside, coarse must mean rude.

A Tell how the highlighted words in each sentence are related. Choose types of analogies from the word bank below.

synonyms	category	object to function
antonyms	part to whole	

1. The crab fishers will catch king crabs in big traps.

   _____

2. Stella's baby brother won't go to sleep without his bunny, his bottle, and his blanket. _____

3. Esteban was weary after cleaning the basement for six hours, but he felt rested after a sandwich and a nap.

   _____

4. Mom took her leather purse to the shoemakers to get the strap fixed. _____

5. When Ken yelled, "Fetch!" his puppy immediately bounded off to retrieve the ball. _____

B Circle the correct word to complete the analogies. The first one has been done for you.

1. trap is to catch as wrench is to   capture   (tighten)

2. bottle is to blanket as robin is to   jay   bird

3. weary is to rested as greedy is to   selfish   generous

4. strap is to purse as knuckle is to   fist   palm

5. fetch is to retrieve as assist is to   help   carry

305

Compare and Contrast

When we **compare** we tell how things are alike, or the same. When we **contrast** we tell how things are different. A Venn diagram can help you keep track of things that are the same and different.

A What are your two favorite sports? How are they the same? How are they different? Write the name of each sport in the diagram. Write about the first sport in the left circle. Write about the second sport in the right circle. Write what is the same for both sports in the middle.

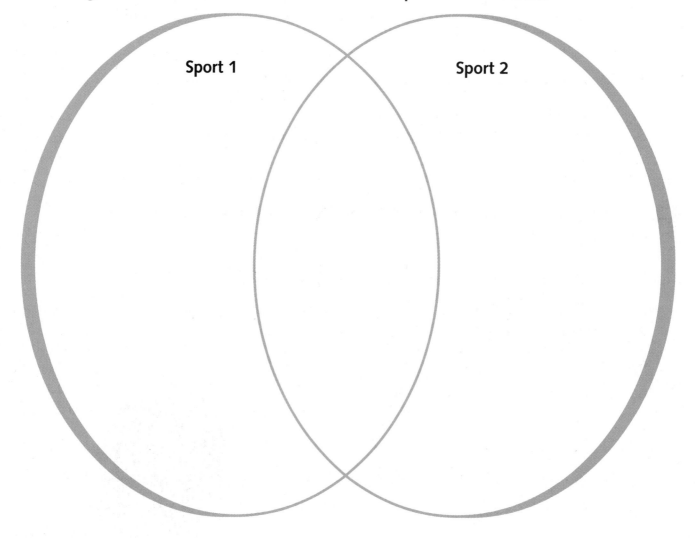

Sport 1   Sport 2

Contractions

Remember, a **contraction** is a short way to write two words together. You use an apostrophe (') to replace the missing letters.

> you are = you're
>
> I will = I'll
>
> it is = it's

A Draw a line to match the two words on the left to the contraction on the right.

1. I am   we're

2. we are   he's

3. you will   there's

4. he is   I'm

5. we will   we'll

6. there is   you'll

B Write the two words for the contraction.

1. she's = _____

2. I'll = _____

3. I'm = _____

4. he'll = _____

5. it's = _____

6. they'll = _____

Inquiry Checklist: Week 2

Put a check mark next to each item once it is complete.

Collect Information

☐ I used the Evaluating Sources Checklist to check my sources.

PRACTICE COMPANION 372

☐ I recorded information from at least one good source using an Investigation Sheet.

4. Organize and Synthesize Information

☐ Each person in my group shared information.

☐ We organized the information using the Chain Organizer or another type of organizer.

☐ We synthesized the information and found at least one new idea.

5. Confirm or Revise Your Conjecture

☐ We used our new understandings to decide if we should revise our conjecture or our Inquiry Question.

☐ We filled in the Idea Tracker for Week 2.

☐ We posted our revised Inquiry Question and conjecture on the Question Board.

☐ All group members completed their Week 2 Inquiry Planners.

PRACTICE COMPANION 309

Notes:

_____

_____

_____

_____

_____

_____

Inquiry Planner: Week 2

Write your group's updated Inquiry Question and conjecture. Then write your Action Plan for next week.

My group's updated Inquiry Question is: _____

_____

My group's updated conjecture is: _____

_____

Action Plan

1. What topics will I collect information for? _____

_____

_____

2. What sources will I use? _____

_____

_____

3. Where will I find these sources? _____

_____

_____

4. When will I collect information? _____

_____

_____

5. How will I record the information? _____

_____

_____

Think Back
Selection 2

What challenges did the person you read about face? How did he or she overcome them? Fill in the chart with your answers.

Challenge	How It Was Overcome

How do people set and meet goals? On the lines below, use examples from your selection to explain.

_____

_____

_____

_____

_____

_____

_____

Focus Question: How do people stick with their goals, even when they face challenges?

Think about the following: *losing your guitar, spraining your ankle before a big race,* and *dealing with rainy weather on the day of the school picnic.* For each example, how would you stick with your goals, despite the challenges? Write your answers on the lines below.

Losing your guitar

_____

_____

_____

Spraining your ankle before a big race

_____

_____

_____

Dealing with rainy weather on the day of the school picnic

_____

_____

_____

Study the Model

News Report

Read the Writing Model along with your teacher. Look for the main idea and supporting details.

Savvy Site Builder Works for Students

by Matt Chen

MILLTOWN—Hugo Ortega is a County School fourth-grader with a mission. A year ago, Hugo started a Web site called Milltown Kids, devoted to getting children involved in recreational and service activities. Now he has clients all over town.

Hugo describes how it began. "When I'd get to school on Mondays, everyone there would be talking about cool stuff they'd done over the weekend," he says. "I hadn't done anything!" So one day last May, Hugo researched local events. He found that he could subscribe to e-newsletters from museums, service groups, and newspapers. He accepted everything and bookmarked events calendars.

"It was too much info," he says. "I wanted to put it all in one place, so I started a Web site." Other students heard about his site, and they started sending him calendar items. Hugo now gets 200 listings a month. "It's worth the work," he says. "Kids are doing more with each other and helping out the community. We're better friends and citizens."

"What are you going to do this weekend?" Hugo asks as a group of students passes. The students shrug. Hugo whips out a laptop. Typing quickly, he opens the calendar on the Milltown Kids Web site. Within minutes, the students have their plans.

"I'm going skating," says Laurel Gordon, a fourth-grader. "I'll go to the park to pick up trash," says third-grader Pesh Hasan. Hugo closes his computer and smiles. His job is done.

Evaluation Rubric

News Report

Writing Traits	Goals	Yes	Needs Work!	Now it's OK.
Organization	The main idea is at the beginning of my news report. My paragraphs go from most to least important.			
Ideas	My news report is interesting to read. I give supporting details.			
Voice	I sound like a reporter who was there. I am careful not to include my own opinion.			
Word Choice	I use strong verbs in the active voice. I include details that tell *who*, *what*, *when*, *where*, and *why*.			
Sentence Fluency	The paragraphs and sentences flow smoothly from one to the next.			
Conventions	All of the words are spelled correctly. I use correct punctuation. I use simple, compound, and complex sentences correctly.			

News Report

Peer Review

Read your partner's paper. Then finish each sentence.

1. I see that this news report has _____

_____

_____

_____

2. Some strong verbs in the active voice that the author uses are _____

_____

_____

_____

3. One example of a complex sentence that the author might use is _____

_____

_____

_____

Name of Reader _____

Avoid Double Negatives

You can only use one negative word in a sentence. If you have two negatives, this is called a **double negative**.

Negative words include the following:

- no

- not

- none

- hardly

- nowhere

- neither

- nobody

- nothing

Underline each correct word in parentheses.

1. I don't want (anything, nothing) to eat.

2. We could not find (nowhere, anywhere) to play.

3. The dogs do not need (any, no) treats.

4. They didn't have (any, no) tickets.

5. I cannot find my book (nowhere, anywhere).

6. He didn't bring (any, none) food.

7. I haven't seen (nobody, anybody) on the field.

8. He never plays (nothing, anything) exciting.

Troublesome Pairs

Some words sound alike, but they are spelled differently and have different meanings. Experienced writers make sure they use the correct form so their ideas make sense.

Troublesome pairs include:

to, too, two
sit, set
there, they're, their
lay, lie

Underline the correct word in parentheses to complete each sentence.

1. I want (to, too, two) see the new mystery movie.

2. Please (sit, set) the table for dinner.

3. You need to bring (there, they're, their) books back.

4. (Lay, Lie) the ropes down on the deck.

5. I am (to, too, two) tired to play today.

6. The ball is over (there, their, they're).

7. I have (to, too, two) new dogs!

8. Buster will (lay, lie) on the floor and go to sleep.

Sentence Structure

Remember, a sentence expresses a complete thought. The words in a sentence must appear in the correct order. Most sentences follow the subject, verb, object order.

Subject = Who or what the sentence is about

Verb = What the subject is doing

Object = Who or what receives the action of the subject

The busy student ate a sandwich.

subject verb object

In each sentence below, underline the subject, circle the verb, and double underline the object.

1. The boy fed the dog.

2. The teacher showed the class a movie.

3. My dad plays the saxophone.

4. The coach blew the whistle.

5. The horse jumped the fence.

6. Thomas ate oranges.

7. Juanita read a book.

8. The girl kicked a ball.

9. My brother builds model cars.

10. Our principal ran in the race.

Complex Sentences

A **complex sentence** has an independent clause and one or more dependent clauses. A complex sentence always has a subordinating conjunction.

Some subordinating conjunctions are: *because, since, after, while, where.*

The students are studying because they have a test tomorrow.

Add a subordinating conjunction to each sentence to make it a complex sentence.

1. We were sad _____ the movie was over.

2. We stayed inside _____ the game was played.

3. Juan and Maria went to the park _____ they finished their homework.

4. Many students visited the museum _____ they wanted to see the science exhibit.

5. The teachers played music _____ everyone was quiet.

6. Maureen couldn't go to the concert _____ she had to baby-sit.

7. It was my favorite restaurant _____ it served my favorite dish.

8. You stand over there _____ I stand over here.

Using Test-Taking Strategies

Read this sample test question based on *Reaching Your Goals.*

What must you do to reach a goal?

- (A) Think about what I want to do
- (B) Practice very little
- (C) Work really hard at what I want to achieve
- (D) Show people what I want to do

Think carefully about each answer choice:

- Is (A) a possible answer? No, this is not how you reach a goal.

- Is (B) a possible answer? No, look on page 446. The note next to the photo says the girls practice hard to play their instruments.

- Is (C) a possible answer? Look on page 449. It says to reach your goal you have to strive and work really hard.

- Is (D) a possible answer? No, this is not how you reach a goal.

Think carefully about each answer choice. Then check to see what the chapter says to find the correct answer. In this case, C is the answer.

Applying Test-Taking Strategies

Here are more questions to answer. Look carefully at each answer choice. Cross off the letter of any choice you know is wrong. Fill in the circle of the correct answer choice.

1. How did Hannah reach of her goal of helping homeless people?

- (A) She wanted to find food for the people to eat.
- (B) She set a goal of finding a way to help.
- (C) She wanted to find homes for the people to live in.
- (D) She spoke at over 200 events to get people to help.
  (page 454)

2. What did Frederick Douglass do after he escaped slavery?

- (A) He learned to read and write well.
- (B) He used his writing and speaking skills to fight for human rights.
- (C) He worked in a place that built ships.
- (D) He watched the men while they built ships.
  (page 459)

3. What are the rewards for achieving goals?

- (A) Working hard
- (B) Thinking of an idea
- (C) Sense of pride and accomplishment
- (D) Facing challenges
  (page 464)

My Weekly Planner

Week of _____

Theme Vocabulary	This week's words:
Differentiated Vocabulary	This week's words:
Comprehension Strategy and Skill	This week's comprehension strategy: This week's comprehension skill:
Vocabulary Strategy	This week's vocabulary strategy:
Spelling/Word Study Skill	This week's spelling skill:
Word Study Skill	This week's word study skill:
Fluency	This week's fluency selection:
Writing and Language Arts	This week's writing form:
Grammar	This week's grammar skills:

Word Skeletons

Fill in the word skeletons.

challenge

Definition

When might it happen?

What might you do if you're facing a challenge?

constant

Definition

What is a synonym for *constant*?

What is an antonym of *constant*?

wade

Definition

When might it happen?

Where might it happen?

Examples and Non-Examples

Fill in the chart with examples and non-examples.

Word	Example	Non-example
constant		
wade		
challenge		
determined		
design		
declare		

Words with Unusual Spellings

			Frequently misspelled words	Review words
league	type	ceiling		
routine	women	guilt	found	vanilla
flood	either	receive		tortilla
month	against	wonder	quite	
pleasant	disguise			
meant	magazine			

A Unscramble the spelling words. Write them on the line.

1. drewon _____

2. geaule _____

3. tnierou _____

4. eievcre _____

5. oldfo _____

6. hmnot _____

7. ueitq _____

8. eplsanta _____

9. gecilni _____

10. nteam _____

11. duonf _____

12. ypet _____

13. mewon _____

14. rtheei _____

15. mgzaaien _____

16. stgaain _____

B **Proofread the paragraph below and then rewrite the paragraph on the lines, correcting the spelling, punctuation, and capitalization errors.**

Last monht I read a magazeen article about baseball. It was qite interesting I fund out that in the 1940s, woomen had their own baseball legue. why did they do this Well, since many young men were being sent to war, they could no longer play on professional teams. so the baseball committee formed a women's league. Practice and games became the ladies rutine. i had many questions while I was reading. I wndered what it was like to be a woman playing professional baseball. were there people who were aginst the league Did some of the ladies want to wear a diguse? Did any of the women recive awards i think I will etheir check out a book or use the Internet to answer all of my questions.

_____

_____

_____

_____

_____

_____

_____

_____

_____

_____

Science Fiction

Practice reading this science fiction story to a partner.

The Mars Experiment

by Leroy Johnson

The flight to Mars was scheduled for the morning. Three other astronauts were going with me. I struggled to pack, knowing that I might not return. Because of space restrictions in the Mars Biodome, I had to select only what I could squeeze into two bags. Two bags! I stared at my life neatly folded and tucked into two old suitcases. My stomach twisted into knots.

It seemed just days ago when the mission commander asked for volunteers for the first human experiment on Mars. He explained that Earth and its people—its scientists in particular—had so much to learn from our life on Mars. Only we could learn if survival on the Red Planet was feasible. Would we find water? Would our ventilators allow us to breathe the air? Would we detect signs of Martian life? So many hopes, so much mystery.

The selection process had taken months. Robots and machines screened all of the candidates carefully. We signed our commitments on official documents. *Did I make the right decision, choosing to go?* I knew this could be a one-way trip. But there was no turning back now . . . .

Did you read the science fiction story with fluency? Use the form on the next page to evaluate yourself and your partner.

Reading Response Form

A On a scale of 1 to 5, rate yourself and your partner. Do this for the first reading and final reading, at least. On a scale of 1 to 5, 5 is considered outstanding, 3 is good, and 1 is average.

1. Did I …

Read the words correctly?

Read at a good pace?

Read with expression?

Read clearly for my audience?

First Reading	Second Reading	Final Reading

2. Did my partner …

Read the words correctly?

Read at a good pace?

Read with expression?

Read clearly for the audience?

First Reading	Second Reading	Final Reading

B After the first reading, share with your partner how you thought he or she read, and offer suggestions for improvement.

C After the final reading, answer the following questions for yourself.

1. What did I do well?

First Reading _____

Second Reading _____

Final Reading _____

2. What should I do to improve my reading next time?

First Reading _____

Second Reading _____

Final Reading _____

Make Connections

What does it mean to make connections?

Readers make connections when something they read reminds them of other things they know. Readers make connections to their own experiences, to other things they have read, and to what they know about the world around them.

Why do readers make connections?

Readers understand a selection better when they can find ways to connect it to things they already know.

1. Before you read
Look for familiar words, pictures, or ideas. Ask yourself: What do I already know about this topic?

2. As you read
When you read something that reminds you of your own experiences, something else you have read, or something you know about the world, stop and jot it down.

3. After reading
Think about how the connection you made helps you better understand the selection.

4. You've made a connection!

Make your own connections as you read the passage. Then fill in the chart below.

Night crawlers are big earthworms that can grow up to 14 inches in length. Night crawlers make excellent fishing bait, and many people make money collecting and then selling them. The best time to catch night crawlers is on a cool, damp night. The night crawlers come out of their holes and stretch out along the ground. Night crawlers can disappear into their holes in the blink of an eye, so you have to be quick. They're slippery, too, so carry a small pouch of sawdust, and dip your hand in it. When you get your hand on a night crawler, the sawdust helps you hang onto it.

What I've experienced	What I've read	What I know about the world

Multiple-Meaning Words

Many words have more than one meaning. These words are called **multiple-meaning words**. The meanings can be related to each other, such as *wind* meaning "air in motion," and *wind* meaning "to expose to wind or air." Or they can be completely unrelated, such as *close* meaning "to shut something," and *close* meaning "to be near something." Use the tips below to help you understand multiple-meaning words.

Use a dictionary

Use context clues

How to understand multiple-meaning words

Look at illustrations

Look at text features

Choose the word from the word bank that goes with each pair of definitions. You may use a dictionary to look up words you don't know. Write the correct word on the line.

coach	loaf	cure
beam	cape	glare
organ	scale	frank

1. Definition A: to smile brightly

Definition B: a long, sturdy piece of metal   _____

2. Definition A: a part of the body, such as the stomach

Definition B: an instrument played like a piano   _____

3. Definition A: a harsh reflection of light

Definition B: to stare with anger   _____

4. Definition A: honest and direct

Definition B: a hot dog   _____

5. Definition A: to heal someone or something

Definition B: to preserve meat by salting, drying,   _____
or smoking

6. Definition A: to spend time doing nothing

Definition B: bread baked in one piece   _____

7. Definition A: an athletic trainer

Definition B: a horse-drawn carriage, or train car   _____

Before and After Reading

Before you read your Theme Reader, answer these true or false questions in the left-hand column. Answer them again in the right-hand column after you read.

Before reading	**America's Champion Swimmer: Gertrude Ederle** **True or False?**	After reading
	1. Gertrude Ederle proved that women were just as strong as men.	
	2. Gertrude Ederle was a good swimmer even as a child.	
	3. In Gertrude Ederle's day, women had all the same opportunities as men.	
	4. No one had ever heard of Gertrude Ederle before she swam the English Channel.	
	5. Gertrude Ederle was not the first person ever to swim the English Channel.	
	6. Gertrude Ederle swam the English Channel on her first try.	
	7. Strong currents and stinging jellyfish made swimming the English Channel even harder.	
	8. Two boats went along with Gertrude Ederle as she swam the English Channel.	
	9. Gertrude Ederle ate chocolate while she swam the English Channel.	
	10. Gertrude Ederle's record time for crossing the channel, 14 hours, 31 minutes, stood for many years.	

Author's Message

The **author's message** is what the author wants the reader to think about or feel after reading a selection. In good writing, the author does not need to state the theme directly. Instead, he or she gives readers enough information to figure out the message for themselves.

Read the fable below. Then answer the questions.

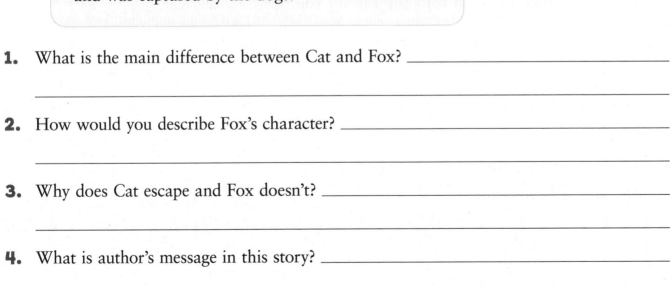

One day, Fox and Cat sat talking about how they stayed safe from enemies. "I have twelve dozen plus four ways of escaping my enemies," Fox bragged.

"I have only one," said Cat, "but it is usually enough." Just then they heard the hunter's dogs barking. Cat ran up a tree and hid in the leaves. "This is my plan," said Cat. "What is yours?"

Fox considered one plan after another. Every plan had good and bad points. The dogs got closer. When they arrived, Fox was still thinking and was captured by the dogs.

1. What is the main difference between Cat and Fox? _____

_____

2. How would you describe Fox's character? _____

_____

3. Why does Cat escape and Fox doesn't? _____

_____

4. What is author's message in this story? _____

_____

Read and Respond

Read the questions. Write your answers on the lines.

1. This story is a biography, or the true story of a person's life. If someone were going to write your biography, describe one event you would want it to include.

   _____

   _____

   _____

   _____

2. List three details from the story that showed how Gertrude Ederle was determined to succeed.

   _____

   _____

   _____

   _____

3. Describe a time when you did something that was very challenging. How did you do it? Did it turn out well for you?

   _____

   _____

   _____

   _____

4. Do you think women get more respect today than they did in Gertrude Ederle's time? Why or why not?

   _____

   _____

   _____

   _____

Text Structure

The way a selection is organized is its **text structure**. One common type of text structure is to write events in the order in which they happened. This type of text structure is called chronological order. Signal words can help you identify the order in which things happen.

Signal Words:

first, next, then, finally

Read the paragraph. Find and circle signal words to help you identify the text structure. Write the text structure on the lines below.

Javier wanted to win the swim meet in May. He knew he would have to work very hard to achieve his goal. First, he began going to his community pool every day after school. Next, he worked on getting faster at swimming his laps. Javier's teammate Michael practiced racing with him. Then, it was time for the big swim meet. Javier's teammates, friends, and family all gathered to watch. The whistle blew and Javier dove into the pool. He gave everything he had on each lap. The last lap was coming and he was in the lead. He pushed harder and harder. Finally, he touched the wall. He looked up and saw everyone cheering for him. He had won!

Adverb Suffixes

Remember, adverbs are words that describe how, when, or where an action takes place. Suffixes are word parts added to the end of a word. Some **adverb suffixes** you might see include:

-ly   *-wise*   *-ways*

A **Add the suffix to the base word. Write the adverb on the line.**

1. quick + ly = _____

2. side + ways = _____

3. loud + ly = _____

4. other + wise = _____

5. careful + ly = _____

B **Write a sentence for each of the adverbs listed above.**

1. _____

_____

2. _____

_____

3. _____

_____

4. _____

_____

5. _____

_____

Inquiry Checklist: Week 3

Put a check mark next to each item once it is complete.

Share New Information

☐ Each person in my group shared information.

☐ We revised our conjecture if our understandings changed.

☐ We filled in the Idea Tracker for Week 3.

6. Develop Presentation

☐ We chose a format for our presentation.
PRACTICE COMPANION 292, 373

☐ We talked about how we might use technology in our presentation.

☐ We created the presentation format.

☐ We used the Presentation Organizer to plan our presentation.

☐ We gave a speaking part to each group member.

☐ All group members completed their Week 3 Inquiry Planners.
PRACTICE COMPANION 338

Notes:

Inquiry Planner: Week 3

Write your group's updated Inquiry Question and your conjecture. Then write your Action Plan for next week.

My group's updated Inquiry Question is: _____

_____

My group's updated conjecture is: _____

_____

Action Plan

1. What topics will I collect information for? _____

_____

_____

2. What sources will I use? _____

_____

_____

3. Where will I find these sources? _____

_____

_____

4. When will I collect information? _____

_____

_____

5. How will I record the information? _____

_____

_____

Focus Question: How do people stick with their goals, even when they face challenges?

Think about your selection. How did the character you read about stick with his or her goals, even when he or she faced challenges? Did the character reach the goal in the end? Fill in the web below with your answers.

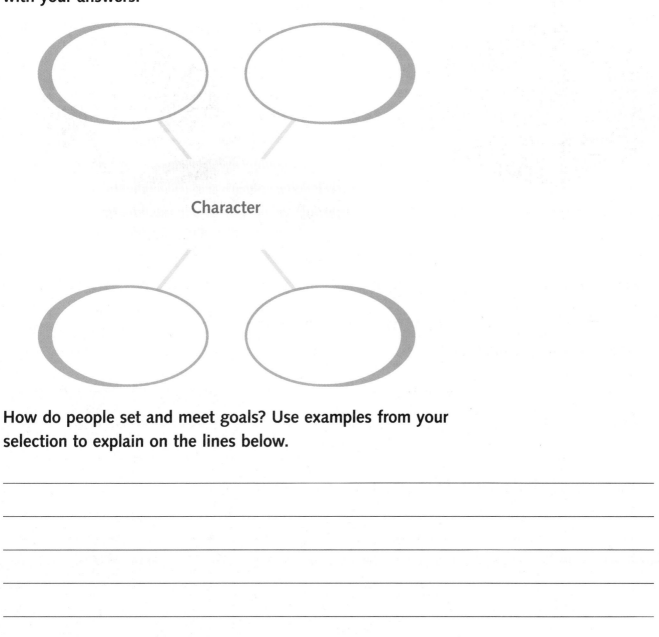

Character

How do people set and meet goals? Use examples from your selection to explain on the lines below.

_____

_____

_____

_____

_____

_____

Focus Question: What does it feel like to achieve something you've worked hard for?

Think about the following goals: *crossing the finish line of a race*; *playing in a school band*; and *completing a school project*. How would you feel after achieving one of these goals? Write your answers on the lines below.

Crossing the finish line of a race

_____

_____

_____

Playing in a school band

_____

_____

_____

Completing a school project

_____

_____

_____

My Weekly Planner

Week of _____

Theme Vocabulary	This week's words:
Differentiated Vocabulary	This week's words:
Comprehension Strategy and Skill	This week's comprehension strategy: This week's comprehension skill:
Vocabulary Strategy	This week's vocabulary strategy:
Spelling/Word Study Skill	This week's spelling skill:
Word Study Skill	This week's word study skill:
Fluency	This week's fluency selection:
Writing and Language Arts	This week's writing form:
Grammar	This week's grammar skills:

Crossword

Use the clues to complete the crossword.

Across

3. The reason a person does something

6. Something that requires using talent and effort

7. To walk in or through water

8. The possibility of great loss or harm

9. To try very hard or make a great effort

Down

1. Continuing and not changing

2. A purpose or something a person wants to achieve

4. Something given or received in return for doing something

5. To run away

Relating Vocabulary

Think of ways you relate to each vocabulary word. Fill in the chart with your answers.

Word	A thing it makes me think of	An action it makes me think of	A feeling it makes me have
1. strive			
2. motivation			
3. goal			
4. reward			
5. risk			
6. flee			
7. challenge			
8. wade			
9. constant			

Words with Unusual Spellings

			Frequently misspelled words	Review words
science	onion	design		
style	rhyme	island	brought	month
guess	through	breathe	teacher	flood
sweat	mountain	submarine		
money	feather			
plaid	country			

A Write the spelling words in alphabetical order. Remember to include the Frequently misspelled words and the Review words.

1. _____   11. _____

2. _____   12. _____

3. _____   13. _____

4. _____   14. _____

5. _____   15. _____

6. _____   16. _____

7. _____   17. _____

8. _____   18. _____

9. _____   19. _____

10. _____   20. _____

B **Proofread the paragraph. Rewrite the paragraph on the lines below, correcting the spelling, punctuation, and capitalization errors.**

My sience techer, mrs gregorio, is teaching us about the ocean She showed us pictures of a real submarin. I have a lot of questions. I want to know how it moves thrugh the water. How can you brethe on a submarine? how much mone does it cost to build I want to learn how people desine them. what countr are they made in Can they take you to an iland? are they bigger than a muntain? I gess i need to ask my teacher all these questions!

_____

_____

_____

_____

_____

_____

_____

_____

_____

_____

Song Lyrics

Practice reading these song lyrics to a partner.

Frontier of Forever

Adapted from a song by Betty Curtis

Think about tomorrow,
Think what you can bring.
Don't be afraid to shout it,
Don't be afraid to sing!
And if they call you foolish,
Keep singing the same song.
Keep looking to the future.
Keep your ideas strong.

Tomorrow is upon us—
Time to choose your course.
Weave ideas around you;
Hope can be your horse!
If we don't care about it,
If we don't do our part,
If we fear every challenge,
We will surely all lose heart.

So sing your songs!
Follow all your dreams!
The frontier of forever
Is closer than it seems.

Did you read the song lyrics with fluency? Use the form on the next page to evaluate yourself and your partner.

Reading Response Form

A On a scale of 1 to 5, rate yourself and your partner. Do this for the first reading and final reading, at least. On a scale of 1 to 5, 5 is considered outstanding, 3 is good, and 1 is average.

1. Did I ...

   Read the words correctly?

   Read at a good pace?

   Read with expression?

   Read clearly for my audience?

First Reading	Second Reading	Final Reading

2. Did my partner ...

   Read the words correctly?

   Read at a good pace?

   Read with expression?

   Read clearly for the audience?

First Reading	Second Reading	Final Reading

B After the first reading, share with your partner how you thought he or she read, and offer suggestions for improvement.

C After the final reading, answer the following questions for yourself.

1. What did I do well?

   First Reading _____

   Second Reading _____

   Final Reading _____

2. What should I do to improve my reading next time?

   First Reading _____

   Second Reading _____

   Final Reading _____

Ask and Answer Questions

Experienced readers **ask and answer questions** before, during, and after reading.

> When you ask and answer questions, you
>
> - Focus on what you don't understand or wonder about
>
> - Look for answers in the text
>
> - Think about how your own experiences and knowledge can help you

Before Reading

Preview a text before reading it. Look at the title, headings, and pictures. Usually, this preview will lead to questions such as

- What do the title and headings mean?

- Why did the author write it like that?

During Reading

While reading, think of questions that will help you understand the text better. Common questions include

- What does that word mean?

- Why did the author write it that way?

- What are some other examples of this?

After Reading

After reading, you might have additional questions about the text or ideas brought up in the text that you want to know more about.

Before you read the passage, think of questions you might have about the passage. Write two questions in Column 1. As you read, write two additional questions in Column 2. When you are done reading, write the answers you found in Column 3.

Extreme Unicycling

You've probably seen people riding unicycles in parades. Maybe you even know how to ride one of these one-wheeled pedaled vehicles yourself. But can you imagine riding a unicycle on steep, rugged trails? That's what the extreme sport of mountain unicycling is all about.

You need strong legs, strong stomach muscles, and really good balance to be a mountain unicycler. Skilled unicyclists can go wherever a mountain biker can go. They can hop from rock to rock, jump gaps, and even ride along fallen trees. They can spin in place, go backwards, and fit through narrow openings.

Before Reading	During Reading	After Reading Answers
What is extreme about unicycling?		

Use Multiple Strategies

An **antonym** is a word whose meaning is the opposite of that of another word. Antonyms can help you understand what you read. Using antonyms can help you improve your own writing. You can use a thesaurus and sometimes a dictionary to find antonyms for a word.

An **analogy** is a statement that compares two things that have something in common. Analogies show relationships between words. The chart below shows several types of analogies.

- Synonyms, such as *beautiful/lovely*

- Antonyms, such as *light/heavy*

- Part to whole, such as *crust/bread*

- Object to function, such as *brush/paint*

- Categories, such as *paper/pen/envelope*

Multiple-meaning words have more than one meaning. The meanings can be related to each other, such as *clutch* meaning "to hold tightly" and *clutch* meaning "a small purse." Or they can be completely unrelated, such as *fry* meaning "to cook in oil" and *fry* meaning "a young fish," or *rare* meaning "lightly cooked" or *rare* meaning "uncommon."

A Write a sentence for each word below. In your sentence, include the word shown and an antonym for the word.

1. evening _____

_____

2. sturdy _____

_____

3. bold _____

_____

B Use words from the word bank to complete the analogies.

hold	garage	perch
limb	punch	school

1. *bean* is to *burrito* as *car* is to _____

2. *captain* is to *ship* as *principal* is to _____

3. *cure* is to *heal* as *grasp* is to _____

C Choose the word from the word bank in Part B that goes with each pair of definitions below. You may use a dictionary to look up words you don't know.

1. Definition A: a branch on a tree

Definition B: an arm or leg _____

2. Definition A: a place for a bird to sit

Definition B: a freshwater fish _____

3. Definition A: a drink with fruit juice

Definition B: to hit with a fist _____

Before and After Reading

Before you read the next selection, read these statements and put a check next to the ones you believe to be true. Check again after reading.

Before reading	Planet Kids	After reading
	Statement	
	1. Even kids can be leaders.	
	2. It's easier to be a leader if you are tall.	
	3. Children can't be trusted to behave without adults around.	
	4. Leaders need good helpers.	
	5. Without strong leaders, a community gets out of control.	

Before reading	The Write Way	After reading
	Statement	
	1. New experiences are always scary.	
	2. It's important to stand up to people when they tease you.	
	3. People shouldn't be allowed to make fun of people because of the food they eat.	
	4. The pen is mightier than the sword.	
	5. Pretending to be brave can help you actually be brave.	

Before reading	The Salt March	After reading
	Statement	
	1. People have much more power when they work together than when they work separately.	
	2. Mohandas Gandhi was a great Indian warrior.	
	3. People shouldn't tell other people to do things they don't want to do themselves.	
	4. India won independence from Great Britain in 1947.	

Before reading	The Mind-Reader	After reading
	Statement	
	1. It's dangerous to touch stray dogs in the street.	
	2. People who read animals' minds should keep it a strict secret.	
	3. If you could understand the thoughts of animals, you'd find that most of them are grumpy, or sad.	
	4. Animal shelters provide an important service for their communities.	
	5. When you have an unusual talent, you have to be careful not to let others exploit you.	

Paraphrase

Remember, when you **paraphrase**, you use your own words to restate information you have read or heard.

Read the passages from *America's Champion Swimmer*.

Gertrude Ederle was born on October 23, 1906. She was the third of six children and was raised in New York City, where she lived in an apartment next to her father's butcher shop. Her family called her Gertie. Most everyone else called her Trudy.

After that near disaster, Trudy's father was determined to teach her to swim. For her first lesson, he tied one end of a rope to Trudy's waist and held on to the other end. He put Trudy into a river and told her to paddle like a dog.

Using your own words, paraphrase each passage above.

1. _____

_____

_____

_____

2. _____

_____

_____

_____

Contractions

> Remember, a **contraction** is a short way to write two words together. You use an apostrophe (') to replace some of the letters.
>
> I will = I'll

A **Write the correct contraction for each of the two words.**

1. we will = _____

2. she is= _____

3. they are = _____

4. it will= _____

5. I am = _____

6. you are= _____

B **Complete each sentence below using the correct contraction.**

1. Rose won't ride with you to the fair; _____ ride with me.

2. Put the dogs in the backseat; otherwise _____ try to jump up front.

3. Richard said that _____ tired of waiting for you.

4. I wanted to get going soon because _____ always on time.

5. Cynthia and Russell are going to the movies, and _____ seeing a comedy.

6. Pick Juanita for your team because _____ the fastest runner.

Inquiry Checklist: Week 4

Put a check mark next to each item once it is complete.

Share New Information

☐ Each person in my group shared information.

☐ We revised our conjecture if our understandings changed.

7. Deliver Presentation

☐ We rehearsed our presentation.

☐ We presented for another group.

☐ We used the Presentation Rubric to evaluate our own presentation.

☐ We used the Presentation Rubric to evaluate the other group's presentation.

☐ We received feedback. We used the Presentation Organizer to revise our presentation.

Identify New Questions

☐ All group members listed new questions on their Week 4 Inquiry Planners.

PRACTICE COMPANION 357

☐ We posted new questions on the Question Board.

Notes:

_____

_____

_____

_____

_____

_____

_____

Inquiry Planner: Week 4

Write your new questions and your plans for finding out more.

1. What other questions do I have? _____

   _____

   _____

   _____

2. What sources can I use to find out more? _____

   _____

   _____

   _____

3. Where will I find these sources? _____

   _____

   _____

   _____

4. When will I collect information? _____

   _____

   _____

   _____

Self-Assessment Rubric

Read each goal in the chart. Make a check mark to give yourself a score of 3, 2, or 1. Then finish the sentences below.

Category	Goals	Very Good 3	OK 2	Needs Work 1
Group Role	I understood and fulfilled my role.			
Participation	I helped my group do each step of the Inquiry Process.			
Research	I found information on my own and shared it with my group.			
Listening	I gave others a chance to speak and listened well.			
Collaboration	I shared my ideas and respected others' ideas.			
Responsibility	I stayed on task during group work.			
Presentation	I was ready for our presentation. I spoke clearly and effectively.			
Enjoyment	I enjoyed working with others in my group.			

1. One thing I did well was _____

_____

_____

2. One thing I would like to do better is _____

_____

_____

Focus Question: What does it feel like to achieve something you've worked hard for?

What does the character you read about want to achieve and why? How does the character feel after working hard and achieving his or her goal? Fill in the chart below with details from your selection.

Character	Goal	Feeling

How do people set and meet goals? Use examples from your selection to explain on the lines below.

_____

_____

_____

_____

_____

_____

_____

_____

Study the Model

Mystery

Read the Writing Model along with your teacher. Look for details that give clues to help the reader solve the mystery.

The Case of the Growing Library

by Maddie Baum

Jason waved his arms frantically as he ran out of the school library one morning. There were books piled everywhere! He and his friend, Ana, couldn't understand why a huge stack of books sat in the middle of the floor. It was almost up to Jason's shoulders.

Another friend, Sadie, came by. She wondered what it all meant too. Where did they come from? They had been told their school didn't have enough money to buy new books. Even the librarian, Mr. Hall, scratched his head.

As winter passed, more and more books appeared. Ana quizzed her classmates. She asked friends where they had been the night before and what they had been doing. Despite her detective work, books kept arriving mysteriously.

Then one evening after swim class, the students met for tacos. Sadie yawned after her second taco and told her friends she had to go. Ana narrowed her eyes as she watched her leave, and then she said to Jason, "Come on!" They crept into the evening fog.

On Baker Street, they watched Sadie walk past her house and ring a neighbor's doorbell. Then another one. And another. Each time, she carefully put something into a bag. Finally, Ana and Jason got close enough to hear. Sadie was asking her neighbors for money! They jumped out from behind a bush, saying, "Aha! It was you!"

Sadie nodded and smiled. Then she asked her friends if they wanted to help. After all, she told them, the bookstore closed in an hour.

Evaluation Rubric

Mystery

Writing Traits	Goals	Yes	Needs Work!	Now it's OK.
Organization	I present a problem or puzzle at the beginning of the story. I sequence clues logically. I solve the mystery by the end of the story.			
Ideas	My mystery has an interesting setting and realistic characters. I include details that give clues to the ending.			
Voice	My mystery has suspense and surprise. I provide details that will capture my readers' attention.			
Word Choice	I use descriptive language to describe my setting and create mood.			
Sentence Fluency	I vary sentence structure.			
Conventions	I use correct punctuation. The appositive phrases modify the correct words. All the words are spelled correctly. I use simple, compound, and complex sentences correctly.			

Mystery

Peer Review

Read your partner's paper. Then finish each sentence.

1. I see that in this mystery, _____

_____

_____

_____

2. Some words that make the story suspenseful are _____

_____

_____

_____

3. One example of an appositive phrase that the author might use is _____

_____

_____

_____

Name of Reader _____

Sentence Structure

Remember, the words in a sentence must appear in the correct order. Most sentences follow the subject, verb, object order.

Subject = Who or what the sentence is about

Verb = What the subject is doing

Object = Who or what receives the action of the subject

The black dog chased the ball.

subject   verb   object

In each sentence below, underline the subject, circle the verb, and double underline the object.

1. The boy raised his hand.

2. My sister plays the piano.

3. Our friends built a tree house.

4. Mr. Diaz moved the car.

5. Dennis made lemonade.

6. The cat watched the bird.

7. Liza baked sweet bread.

8. The dentist checked my teeth.

9. Octavio planted a garden.

10. Stefan rides his bike.

Complex Sentences

> Remember, a **complex sentence** has an independent clause and one or more dependent clauses. A complex sentence always has a subordinating conjunction.
>
> Some subordinating conjunctions are *because, since, after, while, where.*
>
> **The teams are practicing because the tournament starts tomorrow.**

Add a subordinating conjunction to each sentence to make a complex sentence.

1. We were happy _____ school started.

2. We watched the teacher _____ we were listening to the directions.

3. Lyla and Sante went fishing _____ they finished the game.

4. Many parents came to school _____ their children were in the class play.

5. Jeena hasn't climbed the tree _____ she went to the park last summer.

6. Sam missed practice all week _____ he was sick.

7. I will come to the game _____ I complete my homework.

8. Justine cleaned the floor _____ Alex emptied the dishwasher.

Participipial Phrases

A participle is a verb used to describe a noun. **Participial phrases** include a participle plus any additional descriptive words. Participial phrases can appear at the beginning, in the middle, or at the end of a sentence.

The present participial phrase uses an *-ing* form of a verb:

> *While walking to school this morning*, I saw a rainbow.

The past participial phrase uses an *-ed* form of a verb:

> Jocelyn's conclusion, *based on her reading*, was that the author was highly intelligent.

Underline the participial phrase in each sentence.

1. While eating breakfast, I heard the doorbell ring.

2. While talking to my friend outside, I found a shiny rock.

3. When jumping the gate, Roxy hurt her paw.

4. Tired and hungry, the girl called for her mother.

5. The boy wearing the red hat is my cousin.

6. The student earning the highest grade will get an award.

7. Having kicked the ball, Taryn scored a goal.

8. While playing outside, I saw a bird's nest.

Appositives

An **appositive** is a noun or noun phrase that identifies another noun right beside it. You must use commas to set the appositive apart, if the sentence can be understood without it, when it appears in the middle of a sentence.

Karin, my good friend, let me borrow her favorite book.

Karin = noun

my good friend = appositive

Write the appositive in each sentence on the line.

1. Juan, an excellent speller, won the school spelling bee. _____

_____

2. Yellowstone, America's first National Park, is my favorite place to

visit on vacation. _____

_____

3. The insect, a large spider, is building a web outside the window. _____

_____

4. Mr. Thomas, our music teacher, is taking our class to the orchestra

performance. _____

_____

5. Scooter, our family dog, likes to chase tennis balls. _____

_____

6. Darius, the president of our class, gave a speech to the entire school. _____

_____

Using Test-Taking Strategies

Sometimes, instead of choosing an answer to a test question, you must write your own answer. Here is a sample question based on *America's Champion Swimmer.*

Sample Question:
What happened after Trudy won her first big race at the age of 15?

Look carefully at what the question asks you to do:

- You must describe what happens after Trudy won her first big race.

- You must give information to support, or back up, your answer.

There are different ways to answer this question. Here are some possible answers:

- Trudy wanted to swim seventeen miles from Manhattan to New Jersey. She worked hard and beat the men's record.

- Trudy set a goal to become the first woman to swim from Manhattan to New Jersey. Her sister followed her in a boat. After seven hours of swimming, Trudy beat the men's record.

When you must write your own answer, pay attention to what the question asks. Be sure that you do everything the question asks you to do.

Applying Test-Taking Strategies

Now read the direction below. Read carefully in order to understand what you are being told to do.

Describe how Trudy achieved her ultimate goal to swim the English Channel.

Use information from *America's Champion Swimmer* to fill in the chart below to help answer the question above. One idea is given.

How Trudy achieved her goal
Trudy trained intensively for the challenge of swimming the English Channel.

Use the ideas in the chart to write your answer to the question at the top of the page. Write your answer on a separate sheet of paper. Make sure that you do everything the question asks.

Inquiry Process

1. Generate Ideas and Questions

- Brainstorm Questions

- Decide on a Question

2. Make a Conjecture

3. Make Plans to Collect Information/ Collect Information

4. Organize and Synthesize Information

5. Confirm or Revise Your Conjecture

6. Develop Presentation

- Choose a Format

- Organize Presentation

7. Deliver Presentation

- Rehearse Presentation

- Deliver and Critique Presentation

- Revise Presentation

- Deliver Final Presentation

- Identify New Questions

Group Discussion Roles

Choose your group discussion role for each project.

Questioner

- Asks questions to keep all group members involved in the discussion
    - *"Terrence, what do you think about that idea?"*
    - *"Angel, how would you improve this question?"*
    - *"Melissa, what do you think about the presentation format?"*

- Asks questions to keep the discussion flowing and on point
    - *"Have you all shared your ideas about these conjectures?"*
    - *"Have we made a final decision yet?"*

Checker

- Checks the Weekly Inquiry Checklist and makes sure that the group completes each item

Recorder

- Takes notes and completes the Idea Tracker sheet

- Makes sure that important ideas and decisions are written down

- Brings Idea Tracker to each class to summarize what was discussed the week before

- Writes down the group's overall presentation feedback

Discussion Monitor

- Points out when the group may be getting off topic or losing focus

- Points out when group members are not supporting each other, including
    - students not staying on task
    - students interrupting and not listening
    - one student talking too much and not allowing others to share

Information Finder

How I Collect Information

Read the list of possible sources. Choose a variety of sources in your investigation.

Print
Informational Books
Autobiographies
Encyclopedias
Atlases
Almanacs
Maps
Newspapers
Magazines
Written Interviews

Internet
LEAD21 eBooks
Internet Articles
Web Sites
Online Encyclopedias
Digital Books

Film and Radio
Educational Television Shows
Radio Shows
Documentary Movies (CD-ROMS, DVDs)

Experiences
Live Interviews
Watching and Listening
Attending Live Events

Other sources I have identified:

_____

_____

_____

Evaluating Sources Checklist

Use this checklist to decide whether you should use a source.

	Criteria
Relevance	☐ The information closely matches our Inquiry Question and conjecture.
Authority	☐ The author is an expert in this subject. ☐ The author includes a bibliography. ☐ The Internet address is .edu or .gov
Currency	☐ The date on which the information was printed or posted is shown. It is within one or two years of today's date. (If the source gives information about past events, currency is not so important as authority and accuracy.)
Objectivity	☐ The purpose of the source is to inform (not to persuade or to entertain). ☐ The information is based on facts. ☐ The author gives proof to support his or her ideas.
Accuracy	☐ I found other sources that provide the same or similar information.

Presentation Formats

Read the list of presentation formats and technology formats. Go to the Practice Companion pages to learn more about each format.

Practice Companion	Presentation Format	Technology Format
Volume 1 p. 108	**Magazine Article** A nonfiction article that informs the reader about a topic	• Blog • Wiki Entry
Volume 1 p. 200	**Play** A story acted out on a stage by live performers	• Video • Webcomic
Volume 1 p. 292	**Photo or Picture Essay** A series of photos or drawings that tells a story or explains an idea	• Slide Show • Digital Collage
Volume 2 p. 16	**Mural** A large painting or drawing that shows one or several scenes	• Glog • Interactive Map
Volume 2 p. 108	**Diagram** A labeled chart or drawing that explains an idea or how something works	• Digital Diagram • Concept Map
Volume 2 p. 200	**Time Line** A visual representation of events in order with dates and descriptions	• Multimedia Time Line • Interactive Map
Volume 2 p. 292	**Panel Discussion** A group discussion on a topic in front of an audience	• Video • Podcast • Online Discussion

You Can Use Technology

Let technology help you create your presentation.

- Log on to **www.wgLead21.com**.
- From My Home Page, click on Inquiry Project.

Acknowledgments

Illustration Credits

2 ©The McGraw-Hill Companies, Inc/Luciana Navarro Powell; 55 ©Nova Development; 73 ©Library of Congress; 108 ©The McGraw-Hill Companies, Inc.; 300 ©Artville (Photodisc)/PunchStock; 328 ©Andrew Johnson/Getty Images.

Photo Credits

Cover (tl) ©Getty Images/Digital Vision, (tr) ©Photolibrary, (bl) ©Brand X Pictures/PunchStock, (br) ©Digital Vision/Getty Images; 3 ©PhotoLink/Getty Images; 6 ©Photo by B.C. McLean, USDA Natural Resources Conservation Service; 8 ©Sandra Ivany/Brand X Pictures/Getty Images; 9 ©Brand X Pictures/PunchStock; 10 (t) ©Digital Vision/Getty Images, (b) ©Digital Archive Japan/Alamy; 16 (t) ©Photodisc/Getty Images, (b) ©Pixtal/SuperStock; 18 (l) ©Panoramic Images/Getty Images, (c) ©Image Ideas/Picturequest, (r) ©Photodisc/Getty Images; 20 ©Gallo Images Roots Collection/Getty Images; 21 ©Richard Shock/Corbis; 24 ©Photodisc/Getty Images; 26 ©Burke/Triolo Productions/JupiterImages; 27 ©Comstock/JupiterImages; 28 ©PhotoLink/Getty Images; 29 ©RubberBall Productions/Alamy; 35 (l) ©Corbis Royalty Free, (r) ©Library of Congress; 46 ©Photodisc Collection/Getty Images; 47 ©Getty Images/Photodisc; 50 ©Photodisc/Getty Images; 52 ©Brand X Pictures/PunchStock; 53 (t) ©Medioimages/Photodisc/Getty Images, (b) ©Alex L. Fradkin/Getty Images; 54 ©J. Luke/PhotoLink/Getty Images; 57 ©Brand X Pictures/PunchStock; 64 (l) ©Digital Vision/Punchstock, (r) ©Lisa F. Young/Shutterstock; 66 ©Ingram Publishing/SuperStock; 67 ©Charles Smith/Corbis; 70 ©Ilene MacDonald/Alamy; 72 ©Getty Images/Stockbyte; 74 (l) ©Brand X Pictures/PunchStock, (r) ©NOAA; 75 ©Royalty-Free/CORBIS; 94 ©Goodshoot/PunchStock; 95 ©Neale Cousland/Shutterstock; 98 ©Kai Honkanen/PhotoAlto; 100 ©Comstock/PunchStock; 101 ©McGraw-Hill Higher Education, Barry Barker; 102 (t) ©Trinette Reed/Brand X Pictures/JupiterImages, (b) ©Photodisc Collection/Getty Images; 103 (l) ©Masterfile Royalty-Free, (c) ©Royalty-Free/CORBIS, (r) ©Getty Images/fStop; 108 ©Pixtal/SuperStock; 110 (l) ©Photos.com/JupiterImages, (r) ©Christian Musat/Shutterstock; 112 ©Royalty-Free/CORBIS; 113 ©Doug Menuez/Getty Images; 115 ©Royalty-Free/CORBIS; 116 ©Digital Vision/Getty Images; 118 ©Royalty-Free/CORBIS; 119 ©Creatas/PunchStock; 120 (l) ©BananaStock/PunchStock, (r) ©Ingram Publishing/Alamy; 121 ©Getty Images/Digital Vision; 127 (l) ©Creatas/punchstock, (r) ©Digital Vision/PunchStock; 138 ©John Giustina/Getty Images; 139 ©Getty Images/Digital Vision; 142 ©Image 100; 144 ©Stockbyte/Getty Images; 145 ©Getty Images; 146 ©PhotoDisc/Getty Images; 147 ©Purestock/Getty Images; 149 ©F. Schussler/PhotoLink/Getty Images; 156 ©Ian Shive/Getty Images; 158 ©Pawel Strykowski/Shutterstock; 159 ©Digital Vision/Getty Images; 161 ©Pixtal/age Fotostock; 162 ©Royalty-Free/CORBIS; 164 ©Andersen Ross/Getty Images; 165 (t) ©Gary Irving/Getty Images, (b) ©Corbis/SuperStock; 166 ©Stockbyte/Getty Images; 167 ©JupiterImages/Comstock Premium/Alamy; 170 ©MedioImages/SuperStock; 182 ©TongRo Image Stock/Alamy; 186 ©Design Pics/AGE Fotostock; 187 ©Tony Sweet/Getty Images; 190 ©Royalty-Free/CORBIS; 192 ©Digital Vision/Getty Images; 193 ©imagebroker/Alamy; 194 ©Photograph courtesy USGS Center for Coastal Geology; 195 ©Brand X Pictures/PunchStock; 200 (t) ©Getty Images, (cl) ©Photodisc/Alamy, (cr) ©PhotoLink/Getty Images, (b) ©Pixtal/SuperStock; 202 (l) ©J. Luke/PhotoLink/Getty Images, (r) ©Royalty-Free/Corbis; 204 ©Pixtal/age Fotostock; 205 ©Getty Images/Blend Images; 208 ©Digital Vision Ltd.; 210 ©American Images, Inc./Getty Images; 211 ©Mel Curtis/Getty Images; 212 ©Henrik Weis/Getty Images; 213 ©U.S. Geological Survey/HVO; 219 (l) ©Fribus Ekaterina/Shutterstock, (c) ©Digital Stock/Corbis, (r) ©William Albert Allard/Getty Images; 230 ©Carol Wolfe; 231 ©Comstock Images/Alamy; 234 ©Royalty Free/Corbis; 236 ©Tanya Constantine/Getty Images; 237 ©Brand X Pictures/PunchStock; 238 ©Spike Mafford/Getty Images; 239 ©Photodisc/Getty Images; 248 (l) ©Photodisc/Getty Images, (c) ©Alamy, (r) ©Digital Vision/Getty Images; 250 ©imagebroker/Alamy; 251 ©Brand X Pictures/PunchStock; 254 ©Robert Glusic/Getty Images; 256 ©Bruce Laurance/The Image Bank/Getty Images; 257 ©LMR Group/Alamy; 258 ©JGI/Getty Images; 259 ©Digital Vision/PunchStock; 278 © Blend Images/Getty Images; 279 ©Blend Images/Getty Images; 282 ©Elva Dorn/Alamy; 284 ©The McGraw-Hill Companies, Inc./Ken Karp; 285 ©Photodisc/Getty Images; 286 ©Trajano Paiva/Alamy; 287 ©Creatas/PunchStock; 292 (t) ©The McGraw-Hill Companies, Inc./Andy Resek, (b) ©Pixtal/SuperStock; 294 (l) ©Nicole Hill/Getty Images, (c) ©Digital Vision/Getty Images, (r) ©The McGraw-Hill Companies, Inc./Andrew Resek; 297 (t) ©Comstock/JupiterImages, (b) ©Thinkstock/Corbis; 302 ©Comstock Images/Alamy; 303 ©Photo by Lynn Betts, USDA Natural Resources Conservation Service; 304 ©Digital Vision/Getty Images; 305 ©Ryan McVay/Getty Images; 311 (l) ©The McGraw-Hill Companies, Inc., (r) ©Getty Images; 322 ©Jim Cummins/Taxi/Getty Images; 323 ©Digital Vision/Getty Images; 326 ©Stock Trek/Getty Images; 329 ©The McGraw-Hill Companies, Inc./Ken Cavanagh; 330 ©Ariel Skelley/Blend Images/Getty Images; 331 ©Corbis Premium RF/Alamy; 333 ©Royalty-Free/CORBIS; 340 (l) ©Jim Cummins/Taxi/Getty Images, (r) ©IT Stock Free; 342 ©Nicole Hill/Getty Images; 343 ©TIMOTHY A. CLARY/AFP/Getty Images; 346 ©Getty Images; 348 ©Blend Images/Getty Images; 349 ©Ingram Publishing/Fotosearch; 350 ©Image Source/Getty Images; 351 ©Mark D. Phillips/AFP/Getty Images.